A Walk in the Dream Time
Growing up in old St. John's

by Harold Horwood

A Walk in the Dream Time
Growing up in old St. John's

by Harold Horwood

killick press
an imprint of Creative Publishers

St. John's, Newfoundland
1997

© 1997, Harold Horwood

THE CANADA COUNCIL | LE CONSEIL DES ARTS
FOR THE ARTS | DU CANADA
SINCE 1957 | DEPUIS 1957

We acknowledge the support of the Canada Council for the Arts for our publishing program

All rights reserved. No part of this work covered by the copyrights hereon may be reproduced or used in any form or by any means —graphic, electronic or mechanical—without the prior written permission of the publisher. Any requests for photocopying, recording, taping or information storage and retrieval systems of any part of this book shall be directed in writing to the Canadian Reprography Collective, 214 King Street West, Suite 312, Toronto, Ontario M5H 2S6.

∝ Printed on acid-free paper

Cover design: David Peckford

Published by
KILLICK PRESS
a Creative Book Publishing imprint
A Robinson-Blackmore Printing & Publishing associated company
P.O. Box 8660, St. John's, Newfoundland A1B 3T7

First printing, July 1997
Second printing, February 1998

Printed in Canada by:
ROBINSON-BLACKMORE PRINTING & PUBLISHING

Canadian Cataloguing in Publication Data

Horwood, Harold, 1923-

    A Walk in the dreamtime
    ISBN 1-895387-83-3

1. Horwood, Harold, 1923- — Childhood and youth   2. St. John's (Nfld.) — Social life and customs.   I. Title.

FC2196.26.H67A3   1997   971.8'102'092   C97-950155-5
F1124.5.S14H67   1997

*For all the children, now old men and women,
whom I loved in my youth.*

Preface

The people who helped with historical material, from Carbonear and early St. John's, are no longer living. Those included my father and my Aunt Lillian, and to a lesser extent my grandfather, Captain John Horwood. It remains to thank the City of St. John's Archives and Memorial University of Newfoundland for the use of their photographs.

Chapter 1

The house on Campbell Avenue, a large, gracious-looking bungalow built by my grandfather, is standing today, finer than when he built it three years before I was born under its gabled roof. My brother's grandchildren are the fifth generation of Horwoods to gaze through the gold leaf of the lettering on the lintel light above the front door, wondering, perhaps, at its curious inscription, *Kalmia*.

Captain John Horwood chose this name for his house not because he cared particularly for the small kalmia that grows so plentifully in Newfoundland—a kind of poor relation to the beautiful American mountain laurel—but because he liked the sound of the word, and because no one else had a house by that name. He wasn't the kind of man to call his place "The Willows" or "The Poplars" though the kind of things he planted were conventional enough: Persian lilacs and Norway maples which still flourish there more than a half century after his death.

My grandfather had not finished the house when he left it for the last time in a teak box with silver handles. The sons and grandsons for whom he had planned its seven bedrooms had departed, leaving him with little incentive to complete his work. After his marriage, my brother Charles returned to live there, and to raise his own children in the house. It is still beautiful, but is now surrounded by urban traffic and exhaust fumes.

Newfoundland's capital in the 1920s and 1930s bore little resemblance to the urban metropolis that it is today. St. John's was a small city of some 30,000 to 40,000, but it had a great opinion of itself:

gateway to the New World, centre of international trade long before the Pilgrim Fathers landed in America, capital of Britain's oldest colony, and also a modern trading centre of some consequence, its shipping plying in and out of every major port in the North and South Atlantic, the Mediterranean and the Caribbean.

Though its people were almost fiercely loyal to Britain, they were international in outlook, traders above all, with a close affinity to the people of Boston and New England. The waterfront docks were the centre of everything, and were expected to remain so throughout lifetimes yet to come.

It was here that the great sealing fleet assembled each spring, and sometimes had to saw its way out of a frozen harbour. Here the ships returned, weighted down with pelts, if lucky, and always slippery with seal oil, rancid and stinking. Then, of course, there were flippers and flipper pies in thousands of houses.

It was here that steam whistles and sirens welcomed each new year in a cacophony of noise, here that governors arrived from England to be met on the King's Wharf by the Prime Minister and the Chief Justice, here, too, that visiting royalty stepped ashore amid an extravagant display of bunting.

Here was the amazing colour of the foreign fishing fleets, dories with red and blue sails drying in the sun, barefoot Portuguese fishermen playing soccer, dark Spaniards bartering Turkish cigarettes or blackmarket bottles of vino.

The city rose in a semicircle above the harbour, everything facing the sea, some of its streets so steep that they had concrete steps instead of sidewalks. Water Street was paved with stone over which iron-rimmed cartwheels clattered with perpetual din, punctuated by the cracking of whips. Flocks of house sparrows scavenged undigested oats from the piles of horse manure.

When I was a child some downtown streets still had stone-paved crossings raised slightly above the dust and mud, making it possible for pedestrians on Queen's Road, Gower Street, and a few other places, to cross without soiling their shoes. At one time crossing sweepers—boys with brooms—had kept them clean and were rewarded by the occasional penny dropped into their hands by the high and mighty, but by the time I began roaming the downtown the sweepers had all retired. My father remembered them from his own youth.

He told me of another employment for children when he was a young man. The bakeries, of which there were four at the time, hired gangs of boys to knead the bread with their bare feet—an ancient custom: in the time of the Pharaohs the Egyptians had their bread kneaded and their wine grapes pressed by boys who worked in the nude.

The city was a hive of small industry, with five or six thousand people working in factories. There were sail making shops, two carriage factories, furniture factories, four foundries making stoves, nails and ships' hardware, three breweries, four biscuit factories, soft drink bottling plants, a huge tobacco factory, plants making boots and shoes, the long, impressive-looking ropewalk where cordage was produced for ships and trap boats, one or two margarine factories, woodworking and planing mills, one of which stood at the head of the Hill of Chips, between Duckworth Street and Water Street East. There was a factory for making paints and varnishes, one for curing sealskins and rendering seal oil for export, a harness maker's shop where leather was stitched and sewn, one or more sheet metal shops making kettles and stovepipes and so on, and four clothing factories employing about five hundred people. In addition to several private machine shops, there were the drydock and railway machine shops where they could fabricate everything from a marine crankshaft to a steam boiler. Coal gas was made and piped around the city. Electricity was generated by water power in nearby Tors Cove, Seal Cove and Petty Harbour.

The generating plant at Petty Harbour had been built expressly to provide power for the electric street cars, which had started running in 1900, and lasted less than half a century. They ran from the extreme west end of Water Street along Water and Duckworth to Military Road and Queen's Road, to rejoin Water Street via Adelaide. Spur lines ran on Harvey Road and Hamilton Avenue. Riding them seemed to me a very strange experience. These self-propelled machines ran without an engine, so it seemed, and kept clanging bells to warn people of their approach. Not one of them was ever involved in a fatal accident.

From where we lived a one-mile walk took you to the waterfront. The Southside was two miles, Cabot Tower three. About the same distance west brought you to Bowring Park, with its great swimming pool in a section of the Waterford River, tennis courts, a mile of walking trails among trees and shrubs and flowers, the big Bungalow where you could pig out on ice cream and junk food, and the boat pond where you could row about in heavy wooden boats or feed the swans. Bowring Park did much to make St. John's a liveable city. The other parks—Bannerman and Victoria—were much smaller, used mostly by people who lived near them.

There were other large open areas inside the city—Buckmaster's Field, a great wedge of empty and slightly hilly land between LeMarchant and Pennywell Roads, with here and there a patch of bedrock coming through the sod. When a circus came to town (a great event indeed!) that's where it set up. Lester's Field, southwest of Mundy Pond, was larger and flatter, and parts had been levelled further to make it suitable for aircraft, which were still making pioneer flights across the Atlantic. Lester's field had an open run of some five hundred yards, and nothing taller than a power pole nearby. Both those large open areas—almost commons—were grabbed by the military during the Second World War, built over, and subsequently turned to either housing or industrial use.

There were still relics of the days when St. John's was one of the outposts of empire, and Newfoundland was indeed a "fortress isle" badly defended by inadequate numbers of British troops. Some of the roads in the east end had been built by defence forces in the eighteenth and nineteenth centuries: King's Road that ran north from King's Wharf to Fort William (near what is now Hotel Newfoundland);

Military Road that ran westward through the woods and across The Barrens to Fort Townsend. West of the fort was the Parade Ground, from which Parade Street got it's name. The CLB Armoury, which included the largest hall in St. John's, was built so that it adjoined the Parade Ground. The Anglican Church, owners of the Church Lads Brigade and the armoury, made it available for exhibitions, fairs, and indoor sporting events. It was big enough for indoor track meets. Memorial University College was built on the Parade Ground in 1925, but a lot of open space remained there.

There was no airport at St. John's until 1941. Small planes flew off Lester's Field or Quidi Vidi Lake, or occasionally off Bay Bulls Big Pond from which I made my own first flight in a Norseman. In the early 1930s small planes would take up joy riders, $5 for fifteen minutes, and we watched, fascinated, as they did dives and loops and side slips to give their riders a thrill. Sometimes they scattered advertising leaflets over city streets, and small boys rushed to pick them up by the armload, defeating the advertisers' intentions.

A German daredevil named Urban Diteman landed his small open-cockpit monoplane at Lester's Field in 1929 and announced his intention to fly the Atlantic. Andrew took me to see the airplane—the first time I had seen one close up. Two days later Diteman took off from Harbour Grace and vanished without a trace.

Arthur Sullivan and Douglas Fraser flew a Gipsy Moth off Quidi Vidi, and Fraser later flew a Curtis Robin monoplane. Sullivan flew the first air mails from St. John's to ice-bound ports along the Northeast Coast in winter as far as St. Anthony. Along with a doctor from the Grenfell Mission, he was killed on May 30, 1932, when his Gipsy Moth crashed into the sea near St. Anthony. Fraser, meanwhile, had lost a plane through the ice at Wigwam Pond near Grand Falls. He escaped unhurt, flew most of the early air ambulance flights bringing acutely ill patients to hospital in St. John's, and ended his career as advisor to the allied governments during the Second World War.

In the late 1930s there was also a gliding club at St. John's. They owned a kite-like glider which they flew off Lester's Field. It was rather marvellous to see this silent machine—a mere framework with a wing—floating like a gull over the city. We also saw the great dirigible airship Hindenburg cruising over St. John's at an altitude of just a few hundred feet on one of her voyages between Germany and New York, where, a few months later, she ended her career in a great fireball of hydrogen gas touched off by static electricity.

Despite such technological marvels from the outside world, the St. John's of the 1930s bore many resemblances to the London of Charles Dickens. There was even child labour at places like the Ropewalk, though the children who worked there never suffered the brutalities of factory labour in Dickens's time. So far as I could tell, the working poor at Mundy Pond, where the Ropewalk people lived, were happy with their lives and proud of their work. They did a fair bit of dancing and drinking, and even for a while had their own regatta on the spacious waters of Mundy Pond, organized by St. Theresa's parish.

There was a plant near the west end of the harbour manufacturing and distributing coal gas through underground pipes to customers in the downtown area. Some of our friends had gas stoves in their kitchens. A generation earlier gas had been distributed for lighting. Businesses and living rooms were lit by gas jets, and there were street lamps, with a lamplighter who ran from post to post turning on and lighting the jets at dusk. Though coal gas was no longer used for illumination when I was a child, the expression "to run like a lamplighter" was common.

Top hats were worn on formal occasions; bowlers were in everyday use. Long-stemmed clay pipes lay in department store windows, exactly like those smoked by soldiers the world over in the nineteenth century. People who considered themselves "upper class" carried little engraved calling cards, just like in an English novel.

Live entertainments, concerts, lectures, plays, filled the public halls. The Vienna Boys' Choir sang at Pitts Memorial Hall. So did a local tenor named Laite on the rare occasions when he gave a concert. There were numerous amateur theatricals, and even, once a year, a Gilbert and Sullivan operetta. Bands played in the parks. People crowded the streets for a parade. I'm not likely to forget the great Labour Day parade of 1938—forty floats, five bands, members of twenty-two trade unions formed in a line-of-march a mile and a half long. I little dreamed, at the time, that I would help to organize the next such parade, ten years later.

People went to the waterfront to see a royal visitor arrive or a sealing fleet depart. They met and chatted on the sidewalks. The streets were as much for social intercourse as for communication.

We had other aspects of Dickens's London less appealing. The large block of old houses, jerry-built following the great fire of 1892, between LeMarchant Road and New Gower Street, bounded on the east by Carter's Hill and on the west by Springdale Street, was a notorious slum, densely populated because it was an easy walk from there to the waterfront, where most of the men, and many women, worked—the latter mostly in the two big clothing factories. Those row houses, with broken windows, leaking roofs, rotting front steps, and two or three families in basement or other tenements, were believed to shelter some five thousand people in conditions almost as bad as those in the London "rookeries" or the east side tenements of New York. The tuberculosis rate was not as high as it was in New York, but it was high enough to cause grave concern, and the whole area seemed to be just waiting for another fire. The fire never happened. The bulldozers finally cleared the worst of the slums in the 1950s.

Perhaps the stable family in its stable background explains why the very concept of an "identity crisis" failed to touch my consciousness until I went to live temporarily in Ontario at about the age of 45. There, for the first time, I heard people wondering "who they were," and the idea seemed utterly bizarre. Was the language being misused? Young people might wonder what they wanted to do, even perhaps what they wanted "to be," but no one, surely, wondered who he was—an amnesiac, perhaps, a disoriented schizophrenic. It hadn't occurred to me that North America might be a society of amnesiacs in which doubts about one's identity would be accepted as normal.

I never had any such doubts: I was scion of a family whose members had always believed they could do anything they wanted with their lives, and as far back as I can remember thinking about such matters—at the age of nine or ten—I knew what I was going to do with mine.

That house so oddly named by the eccentric old master mariner who built it belongs in another place. A spreading white bungalow with dormer windows upstairs and wide, concave eaves like a formosan hat brim, it was designed to give shade in the tropical sun of Barbados, where Captain John saw it and admired it, and decided on the spot to reproduce it in Newfoundland. The interior plan was simple: a hallway running full length with three large living rooms on the east side, three bedrooms and a stair room on the west, upstairs a central hall surrounded by four more bedrooms and a bathroom, a spacious basement underneath, and a back porch as big as many people's kitchens.

Bay windows gave a sense of spaciousness to the parlour and front bedroom downstairs; they did not project into the sun, but into the shade of a wide veranda—a place for taking tea and planters' punch—but what we took there was lemonade in the rare but intense heat of July and August.

From the veranda on a fine day you could see the flags go up on the blockhouse (Cabot Tower) to announce the arrival of a ship off The Narrows. If the ship was flying a house flag—Bowring's or Job's or Hickman's or Crosbie's for instance—the blockhouse would hoist that flag too, so everyone would know, an hour or two in advance, what merchant's ship was coming in. If you watched at the right time you could also see the puff of white smoke as they fired the noonday gun, and then, some seconds later, the boom of its report. As yet there were no radio time signals. House clocks and ships' chronometers were checked against the noonday gun.

The house was, of course, painted gloss white, as further protection against the sun, but mainly because white was the "right" colour for a house. Captain John mixed the paint himself, as he had done when painting his ships, using white lead and linseed oil, then adding a little blue pigment to whiten the white still further.

Though it is as different from the house my wife and I built at Upper Clements in Nova Scotia as a Mexican hacienda is from an English cottage, I am still comfortable in that house where I was born. My father, having lived for half a century in houses of his own construction, moved back there in his ninety-first year. There was something highly appropriate in his decision to die in the house where his sons had been born, where his father had died in 1938, and his mother had died some ten years later. He, in turn, died in that front bedroom, peacefully, in his sleep, on November 9, 1985. A family death room. One of the pleasant rooms in the house.

A stable background. It makes for a vastly different, vastly more assured outlook on life than that of someone born in a rented apartment in a city where his parents are the transient servants of the economic machine. The people of our family were venturers. We went out to far places. My grandfather had sailed to fifteen foreign countries. Even I, later, ventured into arctic snows and tropical jungles. But we always knew who we were and where we belonged. Never migrants or wanderers or drifters, we had a place and a people to whom we would return.

When I think of our life on what used to be called Mundy Pond Road (an extension of Pleasant Street) in St. John's, I think of elegance. In no sense were we wealthy or affluent people. Like most of those we knew, we lived from payday to payday. My father, Andrew, called himself a manager, by which he meant that he had charge of a department in a merchant's business, a job that lifted him above the level of a mere clerk (pronounced "clark"). My grandfather, retired from the sea, had a job in a customs house, and later a tiny government pension. We were the sort of family who, in terms of a later time, would be making monthly payments on the TV and the VCR. And yet, it is elegance that I remember.

That was mainly my grandfather's doing. The gold leaf above the front door was no solitary gesture, but typical of everything he did. He planted a Norway maple beside a wrought-iron gate. Plush door mats lay at the entrances to dining room and parlour. Plush! imperial purple, royal blue, I can feel their texture yet. Hand-painted china chandeliers hung from bronze chains in both rooms. The Franklin stove sat on a hearth of glazed tiles, beautifully laid and decorated. The dining room table was solid white oak with elaborately turned legs. One of my brother's sons fell heir to it exactly sixty years after it was first installed beside the floor-to-ceiling drapes that separated dining room and parlour. The ceilings in those rooms were more than ten feet above the polished maple floors, and were finished in imported hardwood.

There were other small touches: linen table cloths made from Irish flax, not cotton, which is often called linen nowadays; silver napkin rings. Such things were not, of course, disposable. You acquired them once, and passed them on to your heirs—even if, as might happen, the heirs consigned them to a yard sale, and brought plastic replacements from Simpson-Sears.

My grandmother brought with her from Carbonear a cranberry-glass vase that I still cherish. My other grandmother owned a kerosene table lamp in pressed glass. I still use it when the power fails.

The parlour had black satin cushions with hand-painted roses. Sometimes a dozen sweet peas would perfume the air. There was always a house plant in a huge china jardinière. The plant might be nothing special, but the jardinière was an object to be venerated. Oil paintings of sailing ships hung in massive frames covered in gold leaf. There was a clock, pillared like a Greek temple, that struck the hours all night long. In a trunk upstairs, a black dress was covered with dark metallic glitter. In another trunk was a model of a full-rigged ship, its rigging broken, its spars no longer true, created by some departed member of my grandmother's family—perhaps by one of the brothers whom she had lost at sea.

That house was not exactly a place of joy, and certainly not a place of warm and generous love, but it was not a place where the aesthetic sense would die of starvation either. I marvel at such people as Wallace Stegner and Alden Nowlan who came out of absolutely bleak childhoods in which the aesthetic sense was totally starved, and who, despite this, became artists. When I began visiting Government House in Ottawa (during Ed Schreyer's tenure) and sleeping in a room formerly occupied by Prince Philip, I felt completely at home. I could have lived comfortably in the malachite room of the Winter Palace in St. Petersburg which I finally got to visit in 1985. My greatest delight is in things which live and grow of themselves—children, animals, plants—but elegant objects of human artifice please me too. I am glad that they were present in my infancy.

Yet, there was a certain puritanism even in the elegance. No stained glass turned light to magic in our parlour, though stained glass and stencil glass were common enough in the middle-class houses of the time, and even in some of those which had fallen into the hands of the lower middle class, downtown. We had no candles or candlesticks. I think, like stained glass, they may have been considered somewhat "popish." The only art works were the ships' paintings and framed photographs, including tinted landscapes. My family, two or three generations earlier, had come through Wesleyan methodism, and were then in the process of fragmenting into various sects of fringe protestantism. One of my great uncles (whom I never met) was a Baptist minister; my father's only living brother was a Salvation Army bandsman; he was himself a Russellite; my grandfather had no church affiliation; my grandmother, like her monumental brother, Captain Mark Burke, was firmly Methodist, and rejected the modern nonsense of the United Church; her two daughters and her sister-in-law were Salvationists.

The two rooms I have described, with the chandeliers and the Franklin stove, and so on, were *used*, though the kitchen was the principal living room, and we ate most of our meals there at a table that could seat eight people in comfort, or ten at a pinch. It was furnished with rocking chairs, and a long couch on which you could nap in the afternoon or evening if you happened to be Captain John or his son Andrew. But the dining room held Andrew's big twelve-tube radio with which he listened to evening broadcasts from far places. And the parlour held a truly magic object—an elaborate piano on which I learned to pick out my first tunes, and—a little later—to create simple chords to accompany them.

The piano case was of some light, heavily grained hardwood, with intricately carved legs, and a fret-cut front lined with red silk. The tray for sheet music was also fret-cut and harp-shaped. There was a movable stand for a kerosene-oil lamp, clear evidence that this piano was built while electric light was still a novelty. It's a pity that piano was not kept in repair, but was allowed to fall into disuse, decrepitude, and finally was hauled away to the dump. Today, like many other things in that house, it would be a treasured antique, but during the middle years of this century no one seemed to care for old things. Once "out of style" they were replaced by something newer and shoddier and usually much plainer. Things that would now be treasures were treated as junk. Not only was that the fate of the piano; the Franklin stove with its Greek Orthodox cap of bright iron and brass furnishings disappeared too. Not everything went. My Aunt Lillian saved not only such small things as the cranberry vase, but also the oak dining room table which she stored in a back room because it must needs be replaced by a shoddy "set" from Simpson-Sears. She saved the ornate kitchen range with its chrome rail, its attached water cistern, and its elevated "warming closet."

Lillian played the piano with some skill, if not with educated taste. She could play (not from memory, but with the music before her) concert arrangements and variations on popular tunes that appeared, on paper, to have passages of daunting difficulty, and indeed looked showy when performed. But except for a minuet or two her repertoire did not reach to the classics.

I never achieved her level of skill. I picked up piano playing without a teacher, reinvented the common harmonic progressions, discovered the common modulations, the relationship between major and minor keys and their neighbours, and then began taking lessons from teachers who tried to make me do finger exercises! I learned little from my teachers except how to place my hands properly on the keys. The small degree of useful instruction I received was from a correspondence course that included many of the easier pieces from the classical keyboard composers. Eventually I had the sense to drop the piano altogether. I had neither the time, the determination, nor the self-discipline to become a pianist, and had little interest in being a shoddy dabbler at the keyboard. Most of my life I've lived without a piano. But I have been much enriched by listening, thanks to record players and CBC-FM. I'm listening to a clarinet concerto as I write this.

St. John's, the city where I was born and grew half-way to man-size, had started its life as a ring of fishing rooms and merchants' sheds surrounding the harbour. The "room" was a place to moor a ship, cure fish, and build a dwelling house. The city was never founded or colonized; it simply grew out of the fishery in the first decades of the sixteenth century, a full hundred years before the first French or English "colonies" were planted in North America.

The merchants' rooms were places to build boats, to forge iron deckware for ships, to fit out vessels with rigging, and to knit nets. All this was going on when Jacques Cartier visited it on his way to "discover" Canada. In the sixteenth century St. John's was the only place west of Ireland where you could buy ships' gear or fishery salt, or barrels of wine or bales of canvas, or, if you were lucky, recruit needed crewmen.

Whether St. John's was "permanently inhabited" twelve months a year every year in Cartier's time is a moot point, of little importance.

From the mid-1500s if not before people probably wintered there regularly—watchmen, boat-builders, occasionally pirate crews—but it makes no difference, historically, if the town was sometimes abandoned in winter. Its character was formed and fixed for all time long before 1600, and that's what matters. It was an overseas extension of Bristol, embodying the West Country maritime traditions of the reigns of Henry VIII and Elizabeth I.

In the early years of the seventeenth century, if not before, settlement had begun to creep inland from the waterfront, taking over the harbour ridge to the north. On the Southside no such expansion was possible, because it was backed by rocky cliffs. The Southside could expand only westward from the end of the harbour toward what was later Kilbride. So St. John's grew northward and westward over the harbour ridge into the rolling countryside bounded by Quidi Vidi Lake and Kent's Pond and Long Pond and Mundy Pond and Octagon Pond, a semicircle of lakes that would for centuries form the boundary between the suburbs and the wilderness.

When the drift from the outports to the city began (a drift of which my father's and mother's families were both a part) the baymen at first tended to find whatever homes they could as near to the harbourfront as possible, but when they got around to building permanent houses they built them on the expanding edge of the city, on Freshwater Road and Merrymeeting Road and Mundy Pond Road and Cornwall Avenue. So I was born in a house newly built, barely reached by the power lines, and a little beyond the expanding public water supply. While waiting for the public works to arrive, my family sank a well and built a privy.

Here Andrew Horwood and Vina Maidment were married on January 25, 1923, Vina as yet being a virgin. I was born at home, attended by a doctor, after an eight-month pregnancy, on November 2 that year. Vina nursed me for four months, then came down with scarlet fever, after which my father's sister Lillian fed me from a bottle. No one else in the family took the fever, and within a few weeks Vina was well again.

Vina was a very strong-willed woman who, at another time, might have been an active feminist. She disliked housework, preferred carpentry and painting and gardening to any kind of work indoors, and regarded men as morally inferior, with a tendency to stupidity. It was unfortunate, she felt, that most women were born physically weaker than the "fool men." Though she had never made much use of it, she had learned the typically feminine skills of her time, shorthand and typing, and practised them, privately, for most of her life.

Andrew was a quiet, medium-built man who, apart from skating, which he loved, seemed to shun anything that involved physical exercise. He sawed and planed boards and drove nails when necessary; otherwise, he seemed to take all his exercise at a desk or behind the wheel of a car. He had a temper which he managed to keep under control almost all the time because he was determined to live by the precepts of the Sermon on the Mount. He was a fluent speaker who loved standing by the hour before an audience.

In the spring of 1924, while the house was still unfinished inside, it was almost totally destroyed by fire. One of Vina's numerous experiments with poultry went wrong; a kerosene brooder presumably tipped over in the middle of the night. Andrew, awakened by a family dog, found the back part of the house where we slept in flames. He closed the bedroom door and groped his way along the hall to the front, wakening the rest of the family as he went. They escaped unhurt out the front door, but there was no way he could return through the fire to our room. Circling around, he smashed the window, and got us out before the flames went through the roof. It was only then that he discovered he had suffered considerable burns. He was taken to hospital while the rest of us were sheltered by neighbours.

I don't think the fire affected me at all. Six months old, I went out the window wrapped in a blanket, and probably knew nothing about it until years later. But the family was devastated. They'd lost not only the house, but practically everything they owned, including a prized piano and my father's violin, as well as most of their clothing and furniture. Friends and neighbours rushed to their aid with bedding and the like. Andrew soon recovered from his burns, but was depressed by the loss, especially the loss of the instruments. He told me later that the finest gift he received after the fire was a zither, which he called a harp, from the Strongs, a prosperous fishing family from the Southside. Music was the one great cultural fact in my father's life. As soon as the house was rebuilt there was another piano in it, and another violin, and later on a cello. Before long, he had his twelve-tube radio, and sat up listening to broadcasts from Radio City, New York and Newark, New Jersey.

Fires were no new thing in St. John's—the city had been virtually destroyed at least twice—and by the 1920s there was a reasonably efficient fire department. They arrived on Campbell Avenue in time to save the back porch of our house, and some few items of contents. Some cutlery that my parents received as a wedding gift is still in the family. Some of the Carbonear artifacts survived in a partially burned chest.

Three months after the fire Vina was pregnant again, and my brother was born May 7, 1925.

I remember little of the rebuilding, although it went on for years and years. I remember the house first when it was all but finished on the ground floor, and virtually untouched upstairs. I do recall my grandfather finishing the arch to the stair room, and adding the moulding above the wainscotting in the kitchen, forming a small ledge that ran all the way around the room. A neighbour named Butt was his hired helper; I never learned his first name; he was "Butt" to Captain John, and "Mr. Butt" to everyone else in the family. The only room they finished upstairs was a front bedroom for Captain John's sister, my Great Aunt Anne—that and the bathroom—everything else was left incomplete.

I watched the two men using squares and bevels, jack planes and smoothing planes, a set of chisels, a mortise box, hand-powered drills always called "brace and bit," and such now-forgotten implements of the woodworkers' trade as draw knives and spoke shaves. My own feeling for woodworking and my sketchy knowledge of tools stem mainly from those preschool years watching the two of them rebuild the house. I absorbed far more at the age of four or five, just watching, never handling tools myself, than I ever guessed until I began rebuilding my own first house some thirty-five years later.

I have flashes of memory going back a long way. In the earliest I am looking through a kitchen window whose ledge comes just to my chin, watching a motor car pull in beside the back door. It makes a wide half circle to park facing Campbell Avenue, with the passenger door under our window. People emerge with a bundle wrapped in a blanket. My brother, eight or nine days old, is coming home from the Grace Hospital where he was born. I was eighteen and a half months old, talking in part sentences, using a pencil in a clumsy fist. When Charlie was old enough to sit up, I saw Captain John with saw and plane trim the corner off that window ledge because the baby had bashed his head on it.

Toilet training (about then) sitting on a chamber pot in the kitchen hating my mother intensely as she demanded that I move my bowels. The poor woman had a strong anal fixation, and a lifelong commitment to laxatives and enemas. Perhaps a year later: standing in a corner in disgrace while Vina whipped the backs of my bare legs with a switch. A bit later again: getting a licking on the bare bottom for throwing a stone at one of the neighbouring boys.

For Vina, whipping a child was almost as natural and inevitable as breathing. Her father, the grim, puritanical Stanley Maidment, had whipped *his* children. And his father had whipped *him* with a birch rod kept in a tub of pickle until Stanley rebelled against this treatment at the age of sixteen. Vina didn't beat us very often, but, unlike my father's family, she did feel that it was the right thing to do.

The Maidments, my mother's family, were mainly of Inuit descent, though the name was European. The first Maidment, presumably, had been a trader from Europe who set up a trading station in northern Labrador bartering for furs and hides with the natives. There is an island in the remote part of northern Labrador still called Maidment's Island, named for such a "pioneer." Over several generations, those traders married Inuit women until the whole family looked like "Eskimos." The last of those white Eskimos lived at Twillingate in this century, the most striking being my great uncle Andrew who, in looks at least, could easily have been the Chief of the Council of Elders at Nain. Stanley, my grandfather, dark-skinned, with hair like the mane of a horse that never turned grey even in old age, looked more like a Gipsy than an Inuk, and had no trace of the personality of either. Like his pioneer ancestor, he was a trader, and a man with a hard and unforgiving heart.

Many of my very early memories are painful or confusing. There was a stroller, for instance, which terrified me. It wasn't called a stroller, but a "sulkey." Woven from straw, it had two wheels, a strap for securing the young victim, a sort of boom or handle at the back for the parent to push, and a pair of little wheels or casters that contacted the ground when the boom was lowered. The trouble was that it tilted far back, at a terrifying angle, before it came to rest on the little back wheels, and I was always convinced that I was going to tip over backwards with unimaginably horrible consequences.

When I was two and a half, Vina wheeled me around in this thing despite my tears and protests. I remember being wheeled as far as her father's farm in the country beside Leary's River, which seemed like an enormous journey at the time, but was actually about a mile and a quarter from home. It's easy to date this terrifying experience: Charlie was still a baby, left at home in his crib, and I was still too young to walk to and from the farm. A year later, he would have been in the "sulkey" and I would have been walking. I recall only two things about that farm: the well, which had its own little house built over it, and my great-grandfather Albert Noble, a tall, angular man with a beard—the only bearded man in the world of my childhood. He died before I reached the age of three.

The house on Campbell Avenue was heated by stoves: the range in the kitchen, the Franklin in the dining room, and a massive "heater" in the front hall. The heater was airtight, with an adjustable draught, like a furnace, burning anthracite coal. Despite the three stoves, the house was cold in winter. Of course it was not insulated. No houses were. There was no heat in the bedrooms other than what drifted in from the halls. In spite of the heater, the plumbing sometimes froze.

Every morning the kitchen window was covered with great feathery layers of frost, and to see out you had to breathe on it to make a small peep hole. Grandmother Leah was always first out of bed in the winter, lighting the fire in the kitchen range, and heating up the large pot of porridge that she had made the evening before. Charlie and I would climb out of bed, grab our clothes, and head for the kitchen, the only warm spot in the house. We would stand on the couch facing the range, whose flames danced through the draught-holes in front, strip off our "sleepers" and stand naked in the radiant heat for a minute or two before struggling into our clothes. At least, we did this until Vina saw us and told us angrily that we were shaming ourselves.

"If you're going to dress out in the kitchen you should turn your backs," she said. "You don't want anyone to see your secrets—anyone except your parents, I mean. And you won't want your parents to see them either, when you get older."

I had perhaps reached the age of four at this time, and I couldn't imagine why my grandmother shouldn't see me undressed, or why your front, or your "secrets," should be more shameful than your back, or indeed what all the fuss was about. In the spring, when the sun came out, and my brother and I rolled our long stockings down to our ankles, Vina again gave us a scolding and accused us of "showing off." If there was any way to warp a small child's attitudes toward the human body, Vina was well equipped to do it.

The meals in our house were regular and frequent: six a day. We ate substantial breakfasts, porridge made with rolled oats cooked the evening before in a double boiler, with salt and sugar cooked in, reheated, eaten sometimes with molasses, always with scalded cream ("Devonshire" cream as some people call it; in our house raw cream was used only for whipping). I never liked the stuff no matter how it was dressed up; I'll take my oats in granola, if you don't mind; I've never seen the advantage of boiling them to goo.

After porridge, there might be eggs, usually boiled, though occasionally fried with bacon. Or there might be hash, which I also hated, not because I objected to refried mashed potatoes, but because they always added chopped onions which were never even half cooked. Cooked onions I've always liked. Raw onions give me indigestion, and I've always abhorred them. If I ate raw onion hash at all, I'd pick the onions out, bit by bit. The only other food I completely refused was boiled sliced turnips, Newfoundland's favourite vegetable. Nowadays they call them rutabagas, but I still won't eat them, no matter what they're called. They're good food for cattle.

On Sundays, when there was more time for preparation, breakfast was usually something special, often fish and brewis, served with lots of melted pork fat and scruncheons (little cubes of fat-back, fried crisp). Or we might have roasted rounders—small codfish, salted and cured round instead of in slabs. Or corned capelin, occasionally smoked. Sunday was the one day when coffee might be brewed instead of tea, for the adults. I can't remember what the usual child's drink was—probably cocoa, though Vina gave us Postum, or occasionally Ovaltine. Caffeine was supposed to "stunt your growth" if you had it too young, but no one seems to have known about caffeine in chocolate and cocoa. Andrew drank neither tea nor coffee, just hot water with milk, until advanced middle age, when he took to drinking coffee at all hours, including bedtime.

I suppose breakfast and the other principal meals were served regularly by the clock because Andrew and Captain John both worked at nine-to-five jobs. Breakfast at eight. Dinner at one. Supper at six. All on the dot. The dinner hour break in St. John's lasted an hour and a half: 12:30 to 2:00 p.m. Everyone went home from work for that important midday meal, and most businesses closed. Schools had an even longer break: 12:30 to 2:15, giving kids time to walk home, have dinner, and walk back to classes.

Dinners followed a regular weekly schedule. Beef stew with several kinds of vegetables cooked under a pie crust was eaten once a week. "Boiled dinner" with corned beef and cabbage, potatoes, carrots and perhaps turnips, was eaten on Tuesdays or Thursdays. Salt fish or fresh fish was eaten twice a week, usually on Wednesdays and Fridays. Saturday there'd be pea soup with dumplings. With every meal except breakfast we had a dessert: boiled pudding with the corned beef, a fruit tart (never called "pie") with the stew, sometimes a baked pudding with the other meals.

Sunday morning was the high point of the week. Then the air would be filled with bells—first for the early morning mass at St. Theresa's beside Mundy Pond, and the distant booming of the fine bell at St. Patrick's Church, joined by the far-off chimes of the Cathedral (later the Basilica) of St. John the Baptist, two miles away. Then around ten o'clock the lay-abed Protestants were hurried off by the bells of Wesley Church, Gower Street, and the hoarse chiming of the Kirk. The Anglican Cathedral had a beautiful bell that joined the chorus with restraint and authority.

The bells were especially beautiful to us because we did not go to church in the morning to sit through the crushing boredom of a sermon or a Mass. The bells, instead, proclaimed an idle morning in the house or garden, perhaps with a drive in the country or a visit to Bowring Park. Meanwhile the tantalizing scent of Sunday dinner grew ever stronger; the roast beef hissed and crackled in the pan, where it would be basted many times, releasing its appetizing aroma throughout the house. Sometimes, when my brother and I couldn't wait to sample it, and hung about slavering at the mouth, our Aunt Lillian would take a slice of bread, dip it in the juice at the bottom of the pan, and give us each a piece. I'm not sure it didn't taste better than the beef itself. Chopped onions were added to the gravy, but early enough so they came out cooked. There were always mashed or riced potatoes with the roast, soaked in gravy, and two or three other boiled vegetables, cabbage, parsnips, turnips, carrots. We never tasted cauliflower, broccoli, snap beans or garden peas in autumn, winter or spring, because, of course, there were no home freezers, and no fresh-frozen vegetables. Dried green peas might be boiled with a little salt, or split yellow peas cooked in a bag as "pease pudding" and served with butter and pepper.

Supper was much lighter than dinner. The main dish might be macaroni and cheese, or fish cakes, or meat cakes, or fried cod tongues, or a baked dish of some sort, or on Sundays, salad and cold meat, an hour earlier than on other days—I suppose to allow the women time to clear away the meal and change into their best clothes for church, which started at 6:30, and was heavily attended. Church was a social event. Except among the radical fundamentalists, it had little to do with religion. You went to church as a sort of public ceremony, for community singing, to meet your friends and show off your best clothes to strangers. It also provided an excuse for factional rivalry. Papists and Black Protestants tended to hate and distrust each other. But this was partly racial: most of the Papists were Irish, and were regarded as genetically inferior by the English. (Personally, I've always loved the Irish, perhaps the most talented and beautiful people in western Europe.) To a lesser extent, though, there were class and quasi-racial distinctions between Protestant sects: if you were a Methodist, you regarded high church Anglicans as "not much better than Romans" and if you were Anglican you regarded the Salvation Army as "only a step this side of the Holy Rollers."

Somebody (usually Andrew) said grace before dinner and supper, but it was a pure formality, six or seven words, usually rhymed, uttered with bowed head. I rather wonder that my father, who was serious about his religion, and attempted to make a life work out of it, did not question this farce, as I did (silently, of course) even when a small child.

Aside from the three principal meals, there were three others: elevender, pronounced "levender" at 11:00 am, consisting of only tea and cookies or biscuits and jam or the like; four o'clock, tea again, at 4:00 pm, with similar trifles, and lunch, around 10:00 at night. The evening lunch might be a little more substantial than 'levender or four o'clock, and could include something like cheese or cold meat.

The men who worked downtown rarely got to eat 'levender or four o'clock, but in the outports where the men were self-employed and started their work day at dawn, they ate those meals regularly. I'm sure the meal customs came from west-country England in the sixteenth and seventeenth centuries—a place and time where men were also mainly self-employed.

In our house everyone ate at the large table that could seat ten people. This was not the universal custom. As recently as 1983 when Roger Simmons, the MP for the riding, and I were invited to tea (another name for supper) in Grey River on the South Coast of Newfoundland, the husband, his visiting brother, Mr. Simmons and I ate in the dining room together. The women and children ate later in the kitchen. On Labrador in 1949 I had the uncomfortable experience of being served alone in a room by myself while the entire family ate in the kitchen.

While Charlie and I were very young we had our supper early, and were in bed before the adults sat down to eat. Vina often made blanc-mange for us—a kind of milk pudding, not especially pleasant or especially revolting. I'd guess it was made from sweetened milk, corn starch and vanilla essence. Like much that we ate, it was low on flavour. If we were still awake when the adults finished supper, Andrew might come to the bedroom and sing to us. Some of his songs would now be considered shockingly racist:

> Go to sleep, me little piccaninny;
> Mommy's gonna swat ya if ya don't...

Or:

> Did ya ever go into an Irishman's shanty
> Where water was scarce and whisky was plenty,
> A three-legged stool and a table to match,
> And a string in the door instead of a latch...

And there was one that had something to do with the people of the North Shore, including the strange lines:

> And they brought up Clement's Puddy
> After Fogwill's bag of bread.

He sang "Lukey's Boat" and "Jimmie Priddle." The last of these was resurrected in the 1970s by performers who either had never heard, or who failed to understand the second stanza. This was Andrew's version:

> Jimmie Priddle, Jimmie Priddle, did you see John White?
> He's gone out fishin' for to stay all night.
> Jimmie Priddle, Jimmie Priddle, did you see John White?
> He's gone out fishin' for to stay all night.
>
> So you get the hatchet, and I'll get the saw,
> You get the hatchet, and I'll get the saw,
> You get the hatchet, and I'll get the saw,
> And we'll chop the eyebrows off of Sammy Dawe.

The whole point of the song was that John White was a police chief, and Sammy Dawe, who had eyebrows of the sort later made world-famous by the American labour leader John L. Lewis, was his assistant. I believe they were very near contemporaries of my grandfather, so the song couldn't have been very old.

Captain John never sang such frivolities—indeed, I think he disapproved of them—but he knew some old rhymes, including what may have been the original version of the famous King William nursery rhyme. Unlike all the published versions I've ever seen, including some collected by Newfoundland folklorists, it made perfectly good sense:

> King William was King George's son,
> And many a gallant race he run.
> He loved the rich, he loved the poor,
> Had many a maid on a bar-room floor.
> The sons he got on St. John's town
> Are mariners bold of great renown,
> They wear the cap, they wear the star,
> So here's a toast to Billy the Tar.

Grandmother Leah and Great Aunt Anne would both have been scandalized if they'd heard him reciting those verses, especially in the hearing of children—"On a bar-room floor indeed!" Captain John generally cared little whom he scandalized, but he saved his rhymes for such time as the women had gone to church. He never did explain what the rhyme was all about, but it must have come down from his own grandmother's time when Prince William, afterwards King William IV, was in Newfoundland as a naval officer, fathering illegitimate children who, if boys, were taken into the navy as midshipmen, afterwards getting to wear the cap and star as officers.

All the women in our family sang, mostly hymns or sentimental songs like "Silver Threads among the Gold." Aunt Anne sang hymns exclusively; after being a bit of a gal in her youth, she had taken up with piety in old age. She'd once had a fine voice, and lamented that it had now lost much of its quality. Even Vina tried to sing, though she was so tone-deaf as to miss the notes by almost a semitone. She stuck mostly to the simplest melody lines:

> Sun of my soul, my father dear,
> I know no night when Thou art near;
> Oh may no earth-born cloud arise
> To hide Thee from Thy servant's eyes.

That seemed to be her favourite. Its flat, dirge-like melody sounds *very* ancient. The English scholar Samuel Butler argued that both words and music had been handed down all the way from ancient Egypt. The sense certainly seems to accord with sun-worship, either of Ra or Aton, and the tune is the sort of simple chant that really might have survived for three thousand years through several changes of faith.

With four able-bodied women to share the work, the housekeeping in the bungalow on Campbell Avenue was well attended to. My mother, who hated housework, did as little as she could get away with, and spent most of her time mismanaging the children, who required a good deal of bringing up if they were not to grow into savages.

Besides the scrubbing and sweeping and dusting and washing of floors that went on from week to week, there was a great *housecleaning* several times a year. This included taking everything off the shelves and washing them down, taking all the silver plate out of drawers and cleaning it with silver polish, necessary because silver, unlike stainless steel which has now largely replaced it, turns black from sulphur dioxide spewed into the air when bituminous coal is burned), cleaning the bronze and brass with copper polish, repainting the stove pipes with a special paint called Black Dazzle that afterwards filled the house with choking fumes until the solvents had all burned away, and cleaning the stoves themselves with nickel polish, as well as with the regular coats of blacking that they received weekly.

My Great Aunt Anne seemed to be the most industrious housecleaner. She is the one I remember attacking the stoves with the various kinds of polish, and cleaning the spoons with Silvo. She also had a chunk of very fine-grained red sandstone which she kept for sharpening knives. But I'm sure the housecleaning was a generalized drive toward spotless perfection in which all the women shared.

Cleanliness was not only next to godliness, but was believed to be essential for health. "Germs," which had been discovered a century or so before, and were believed to cause most disease, were also believed to flourish in dust and dirt. It is a curious fact, though, that people living in houses such as mine, where the cobwebs are allowed to hang in the corners for five years at a stretch, are almost never plagued by the numerous diseases from which all of us, children and adults, suffered in my childhood.

Chapter 2

Horwoods lived in Carbonear from the middle of the eighteenth century, and probably from the middle of the seventeenth. The family, originally from the English midlands, had settled on the Devon coast by the reign of Elizabeth, and one of them became an early governor of Sir Walter Raleigh's Virginia colony. The Virginia Horwoods were likely the only ones in North America at that time, and the first Horwood to settle in Carbonear was probably a Virginia fishing skipper. At any rate, the family owned a fishing room at Crocker's Cove, the extreme north end of Carbonear, in 1740, but they later built houses on The Marsh, just north of Harbour Rock Hill, where my father and grandfather and great-grandfather all were born. Here the members of the family who weren't at sea or employed elsewhere as shipbuilders did a little gardening, and hauled firewood from the neighbouring forest with horse and catamaran. They were the only Horwood family in what is now Canada.

From Carbonear my great-grandfather, Captain Hugh, sailed to the icefields, seal hunting. When his ship was crushed and sunk by colliding floes, he and his crew took their packs on their backs, walked over the ice to Cape St. Francis, and then around Conception Bay to Carbonear, a total distance of a hundred miles.

Here my great-grandmother, Levinia Burke, died in childbirth in 1870 when her daughter Leah was ten years old. Here another great-grandmother, Mary Horwood, would rise before daylight and have her wash ready to hang when the sun rose. She kept her floors covered with fine sand and would take a broom handle to re-create geometrical patterns in it every day. Here my grandfather's mother, Mary Powell, made oilskin clothing for all her sons, sewing the calico and boiling it in linseed oil until it was completely waterproof. She always kept suits ahead for each of them—one to wear, one for spare, one soaking in oil. She owned what was perhaps the first sewing machine in Carbonear, and sewed suits for all comers at the rate of one cent for each yard of seam. All her husband's brothers were shipbuilders. All her sons, like their father, were fishermen, but some of them not for long: John and Cyril began sailing on foreign-going ships; Aubrey went off to college in Nova Scotia, and never returned to Carbonear; Sam stayed at home and became a fishing master with his own station in remote Quirpon Tickle, and his sons for crewmen. John worked in Nova Scotia as a carpenter in his youth, and later as a shipbuilder with his uncle Richard in Trinity Bay, before Richard went off to found the first shipyard on New World Island in Notre Dame Bay, just south of Twillingate. John's young sister Anne went with her brother to the same shipyard as a cook, and later to the summer fishery on Labrador. Great-aunt Anne was no great cook, in my estimation, but the cooking she would have needed to master was mainly making bread, boiling fish and brewis or salt meat and vegetables, and making boiled duff to serve as dessert with molasses "coady" made from boiled molasses and sugar and a dab of butter.

Later John built his own schooner, the *Lord Kitchener*, in his back yard at Carbonear, with "no man to help him only his wife" as his neighbours expressed it. They wondered how he planned to get the ship half a mile across the marsh and along the road to the waterfront for launching, but whoever asked this was told, "You'll see. On the day I'm ready, I'll hoist a flag, and then you can come and watch."

They built the little ship on a cradle, and finished it in the spring. They had rollers under the cradle, and strong ropes attached to it. On the day the ship was ready the flag went up, and every man and boy, not to mention many of the women, came to see the event, and each was told to catch hold of a rope. The *Lord Kitchener* then proceeded at an easy walk to the waterfront, and floated off before noon, her own flag at the masthead. John sailed his ship to the Labrador fishery, and eventually sold her there when he decided to quit fishing for the life of a sailor.

Captain John got nearly all his education as an adult. When he was a boy, they could never keep him in school, and he was generally regarded as a ne'er-do-well in the making. But as a young man he suddenly became ambitious to command ships. He then learned reading and writing and mathematics and navigation from his wife's father, Captain John Burke, whose sons also became master mariners. Among Captain John's books that survived the fire in a sea chest were Josephus's *History of the Jews*, and textbooks on solid geometry and spherical trigonometry. It was typical of him that he'd want to understand the theory, as well as the practice, of navigation.

His wife Leah lost her three eldest children to the epidemic diseases of the nineteenth century—the first at only one week of age, the second at age four, the third as a teenager. She and her husband were still sorrowing for the loss of their elder children when I was a child. The four next in line, Andrew, Sam, Millie and Lillian, all survived into advanced old age. Lillian, the youngest, was born in 1903, when her mother was forty-three years old. Leah nursed all her children for two years or more.

Having lost two of her brothers at sea on the same day, and having spent much of her life wondering if her husband would return from his foreign voyages, Leah was determined that her sons would not become sailormen if she could help it. As a boy, Andrew made one foreign voyage with his father. After that, his mother made sure that he and Sam stayed ashore. As soon as he was old enough to work regularly she got him a job in a Carbonear merchant house. A year or two later, he went off to St. John's, and worked for a Water Street merchant selling dry goods over the counter. Then the family followed him to St. John's, and shortly thereafter Sam went off to Canada with his bride Annie

Barter, who was later to become mayor of Brampton, and to serve several additional terms on the town council.

The St. John's of my childhood had special features which I didn't remark at the time because I knew no other city. The forest of ceramic chimney pots that rose above the roofs I "saw" only after I had reached middle age. The wrought iron fences were another matter, not all that common, standing like rows of spears along the sidewalks separating the gardens of the well-to-do from the vulgarity of the street. Why, I wondered, would anyone erect a row of spears in front of his house? To keep prowlers away? Perhaps. In fact, there was a report of one young climber who slipped and drove a spear completely through the thick part of his thigh. But it was mainly status. I've seen incredibly intricate iron fences in Europe, some of them gilded. Those in St. John's only succeeded in being ugly, and very expensive. But they weren't all on Merchant's Row (Circular Road) or in the merchant's suburb at Waterford Valley. There was at least one each on Freshwater Road and St. Clare Avenue, owned by upward climbers.

Fanlights over front doors, some with leaded stained glass, were commoner than iron fences. Living room windows often had stained glass, too, usually oblong panes above conventional glass windows, with abstract Victorian designs or conventionalized leaves and flowers. These weren't all houses of the wealthy, either. Professionals and managers, those who had made it into the upper ranks of the merchants' servants, also went in for house display, and perhaps for a certain degree of elegance depending on their tastes.

There was much talk then of people "knowing their place," which meant acting as they were supposed to act in their stratum of society, being defferential toward their "betters" and politely condescending toward their "inferiors." Vina had a lot to say about this. I don't recall any of it from other members of the family. She had picked it up, I'm sure, from her father, who had spent much of his life as a merchant's clerk, first in an outport general store, then in St. John's at Ayre and Sons. My father had led a similar life except that he had moved from a counter to a bookkeeper's desk and then to a small office of his own as manager of a coal and salt department for A.E. Hickman and Company.

So Vina's sons were expected to "know their place" somewhere well below the Hickmans, but well above the neighbourhood corner boys with whom they were grudgingly permitted to play. There was an unspoken assumption that in time those sons would move into some merchant's establishment and become part of the bookkeeping and managerial class, expressing their status in houses and cars and fences like "everyone else."

What Captain John thought of this I never knew, but I do know that he wished his eldest son had followed him to sea and had commanded a ship. As a master mariner he stood apart from the land-based class structure into which his wife had thrust their two sons. Master mariners worked for the merchants, it was true, but they worked as free agents, not as servants within the class structure. It made a world of difference.

By no means are all my early memories painful or confusing. Our house stood on the very edge of St. John's, with a wild meadow sloping uphill from its back door, a lake in sight on the west, and large stretches of pasture off to the south.

The lake, the fields, the meadow were all places where my brother and I, the only children in a family of eight, went for walks with our Aunt Lillian, a very strong and, incidentally, very puritanical influence in our early lives. It would be hard to overestimate Lillian's influence on three generations of children: nephews and nieces and great- and great-great- nieces and nephews by the scores. On the whole, a very good influence, I think. She was a prim but warm person with strong leanings toward the pleasant things of life—music, flowers, small animals, walks in the country, and the simpler forms of literature—an excellent companion for a child, in fact, though Victorian to the core.

The unmarried female in that society—the sister, the grown-up daughter, the aunt—led a most unenviable life. She was a minor member of the clan, subservient, with no financial resources of her own, usually with no income whatever, no claim to any priorities; she must have found it difficult to maintain a self-image that she could care for. Such women took refuge in baby-sitting for their more fortunate relatives, doing whatever tasks the more privileged wives preferred to avoid. And they might also take refuge in religion, or, if they had no ear for religion (as most people do not) then at any rate in the practice of piety and in dutiful attendance at church. It must have been difficult indeed for such women to find any fulfilling role. And yet there were thousands of them, even in our small society, finding somehow the inner strength to survive if not to flourish. They did not, at any rate, commit suicide in any large numbers.

The people who stood out as exceptional in my early childhood were not my parents. Andrew compared with his father was no great figure. Vina, despite her toughness, her invasion of the man's world of building fences and raising animals, did not stand up well beside Grandmother Leah or Great-aunt Anne, or even quiet little Aunt Lillian. She disliked Andrew's family, and was determined to take her husband and children away from it as soon as she could.

In the 1920s and 1930s the neighbourhood shop was still a main food supplier, not a mere dealer in milk and junk food as it is today. Since electric refrigerators were unknown (a few people had ice boxes that served them after a fashion) shopping for food was a daily chore, though the food we ate was not nearly so perishable as it is now believed to be. Any cooked meat kept perfectly well for several days on a pantry shelf. Milk, butter and cheese were happy there, as well. If milk went sour after four or five days, you used it in baking. Eggs were good for at least a month, and would keep much longer in a cool cellar. If you felt you needed ice, you bought it at the door from an ice truck—great cubes that had been sawn out of lakes the previous winter and stored in sawdust inside insulated ice houses. We bought ice for keeping milk, and sometimes used it with coarse salt in an ice cream churn. Why the salt? I wanted to know.

"Salt makes ice colder," my father explained. It doesn't, of course, but it makes the ice melt, thus drawing heat from the ice cream mix. I doubt that Andrew ever understood the simple theory of latent energy on which the freezing of ice cream depends.

There were three shops within half a mile of our house, each with its special merits. So with me—aged, say, three and a half—and my brother Charlie, aged two, Lillian would make the rounds, buying a pound of boiled ham in one store, a bag of Tip-Tops or Lemon Cream Biscuits in a second, perhaps lunch tongue in a third. Many things were sold by the slice, and every grocer had his rotary slicer to cut shavings of cooked meat from great blocks, the slices falling on waxed paper, then weighed, and wrapped in brown paper and string. Cheese was cut with a huge steel blade from wheels that must have weighed fifty pounds each. Crackers, cookies and other prepared foods were shovelled out of bins. String came from an overhead feeder, and paper rolled off a twenty-inch spool at the end of the counter. We often came away from the stores with an immense Mr. Goodbar or bag of Hershey bells. (This was when chocolate bars were twice their present size, and sold for five cents. After World War II, manufacturers shaved them a gram at a time down to an ounce and a quarter, and gradually raised the price until something half the size of a nickel bar sold for close to a dollar.)

Across Campbell Avenue from our house was Barnes's store, a large, disorderly place that always had a molasses puncheon with a pump on top. You took milk bottles there to be filled with molasses. At the bottom of the puncheon there'd always be a thick layer of molasses sugar, and you might sometimes get some of it free, a great treat. O'Brien's store, up the road, was the great dispenser of all kinds of biscuits from glass-topped bins. In the opposite direction was Neary's, bigger and better stocked, close to being a general merchant house. All the stores had half-pint, pint, quart and gallon jugs, with spouts like inverted hat brims, made by a local tinsmith and used for measuring. Many things were sold by measure, rather than by weight. Potatoes, if not in sacks or barrels, were sold by the gallon. All other vegetables were sold by the dozen, or by the pound.

Now and then we walked downtown to the merchant houses on Water Street, a mile away. Here you bought yard goods and pound goods and ready-made clothing, sometimes a bit of hardware—dishes or a hairbrush or a fancy glass bowl, perhaps a teapot for a wedding gift. Unlike neighbourhood stores, where they dropped your money into a cash register, those elaborate places had conveyor systems, with little metal cylinders that took your dollar bills wrapped with counter slips and whisked them magically away to some hidden part of the building where the sale was recorded and the money deposited. Then the little cylinder came singing back along the three wires that held it, to drop your change and receipt on the counter. That was technology for you!

Even more than for her shopping, Lillian was memorable for her walks. With her we had our first taste of the joys of travel. The walks might be across the wild commons toward Pennywell Road where sheep laurel bloomed and ground birds nested, but often to the shores of Mundy Pond—even, once or twice, to far off Jensen's Camp in the wilds of Blackmarsh Road beyond the last outpost of civilization, or to the wonderful Wishing Well in the forested valley beyond the first wooded ridge.

The Wishing Well was an enchanted place at the end of a very long journey (a little less than a mile, it seems, but at the age of three or four that can be a great distance,. It was beyond even the fringes of the city, reached by a narrow dirt road through groves of spruce and fir. Wishing Well Road ran up-country, and eventually joined that other wilderness path, Pennywell Road, but before they joined there was a clearing in the woods with a tiny stream that rose out of the earth—the Wishing Well. The clear, cold water bubbled out of the stones below a mossy bank, and the pool it formed was completely overhung, bowered by the branches of wild cherry and chuckly pear. When Aunt Lillian took us to visit the Wishing Well it was a pilgrimage; we were conscious of being part of a magic rite, as young Greeks must have been if they visited Delphi.

When the sun came down through the branches, dappling the

water with crystal light, setting the moss afire like a bed of emeralds, you knew that the world was a wondrous, magical place. At least once we went there in winter after a storm, and looked at the curl of the snowdrifts, the sculpture of the wind with curves and hollows like breaking surf, incredibly frozen, immobile, the perfect rhythm of motion translated into line and form. Lillian taught us to look and see those things, and to take pleasure in them, as she did herself.

The Wishing Well is long since buried under urban sprawl, its mossy bank levelled by a bulldozer, its waters, if they still flow, emptying underground into a storm sewer, its groves replaced by lawn sods. The country road that led to it is now paved and straightened with curb and gutter and concrete sidewalk under the bleak blasts of winter and the pitiless summer sun. Flocks of starlings have moved in to replace the chickadees and yellow warblers that busied themselves among the branches in my childhood, and the air, once sweet with balsam fir, now smells of diesel fumes and gasoline exhaust.

Spring water, we believed, was always fit to drink, and while growing up we drank it with impunity. We even drank river water without contracting typhoid or amoebic dysentery. When we came, on those walks, to a stream or a beach we were allowed to take off shoes and socks to wade—the nearest we ever came to being allowed to go barefoot until we were old enough to decide such matters for ourselves.

Lillian didn't impart much information on her country walks. She was no naturalist. In fact, I knew next to nothing about the natural world until I was well into my third adult career and met the great field naturalist Les Tuck; no such knowledge came out of my childhood.

Besides *Burgess's Bedtime Stories*, Lillian read to us from books and journals, a children's magazine with a serial story about a dog named Chips, *Winnie the Pooh*, from which I'm afraid I cannot recall a single name, character or incident except that it was, in fact, read to me, and some stories that I suspect were written primarily for teenage girls of Victorian background—in any case, the medium was the message.

Lillian was a calm, affectionate person who was not, perhaps, very curious about the world, and certainly had not the smallest bent for sciences. I remember as an adult speculating in her presence why it was that the rowan trees that we called dogberries bore such heavy crops of fruit in years when we were going to have a "hard winter."

"Why," said Lillian, "it's perfectly simple. It's to feed the birds."

I believe my own kids will have much more vivid memories of their walks with Corky and me—seeing goldfinches and rose-breasted grosbeaks rather than "birds," gathering mushrooms, learning to avoid the deadly amanitas, seeing and even feeding squirrels, otters and raccoons, watching a weasel catch a mouse right under their noses, learning to tell spruce from fir and pine, hearing the life histories of insects and dinosaurs, digging clams, playing naked on the beach—they've had a much more varied and involved experience of the world than I ever had as a child. My son Andrew knew more nature lore (mushrooms, trees, birds, mammals, flowers, insects) at the age of five than I knew at the age of twenty-five, and everything he knew he passed along to Leah. When she was barely three I heard him explaining to her that spruce needles are sharp and spread around the twig, while fir needles are not sharp, and lie flat. A few months later, when we were visiting Cape Breton and having lunch under the trees, she looked around and remarked, "There's a lot more fir in this woods than we have at home."

Among our excursions with Lillian were trips on the "electric train" to Bowring Park. It wasn't an electric train at all, but a self-propelled car, what might now be called a day-liner, and it ran a return trip of six miles from a station in St. John's to one in Bowring Park, where the open-air shelter for train passengers still stood beside the tracks in the 1940s, though motor traffic had put the train out of business by 1930.

The fare, for a child in the 1920s, was five cents (deceptively low until you consider it was the equivalent of a dollar today). Bowring Park was a magical place, where white water cascaded over bedrock, and white swans swam on a quiet pond with their own small house on an island. Here, too, there were boats to row, bronze statues of Peter Pan and the caribou to admire, a slate quarry to explore, acres of beautiful landscaping, and a huge swimming pool where you could watch skilful adults doing swan dives and jack-knife dives from the springboard.

Lillian took us rowing on the pond, sometimes with her boyfriend Albert Holmes, an amateur writer and poet of some skill, then on his way to the United Church ministry. He later issued a very pretty little book of lyrics and photographs, *Bowring Park in Winter*, and, half a century later, published his memoirs, *A Boat of My Own*.

Lillian was much better in her garden among jonquils and stars of Bethlehem and monkshood than she was in a field or a wood. She kept beautiful flower beds, collected and dried her own seed, and allowed us to help. It may have been from her that I acquired a lifelong love of flowers and gardens.

Looking back to the age of three or four I recall her flowers vividly. She grew rockets and pinks and sweet Williams and white morning glories that lasted just one day; she had bleeding hearts and red and white roses. It was a simple square plot in front of a city house, but that garden, where I was caught by Lillian's own sense of magic, had entered the realm of fable even before I had learned to read. My own first garden, created with much toil ten years later, was doubtless a far finer piece of work. It had a sunken area with stone steps, a rockery, a rose trellis, a pool, and vines that climbed to the eaves of the house—but I remember it only vaguely compared to the first flowers of my infancy.

Our favourite walk was to Mundy Pond, where we gave the capes and bays names I have forgotten except for Bark Point, named for a barking dog. Though the lake was doubtless already polluted, we went boating among the islands, and saw much older boys swimming there as nude as young Greeks in full sight of the houses and the public road. Nothing of the kind would be permitted to us. Those were Irish kids from a different culture, where children "ran wild." Perhaps we envied them a little. From the lake we brought home white water lilies that filled the house with perfume. It amazed me that such a flower grew wild, and could be had for the taking.

Though Lillian could row a boat, she couldn't sail one, or drive a car, or swim. She milked a cow, ran a cream separator, baked with skill and enthusiasm, could cook an excellent dinner, and was good at embroidery. She showed no wish to travel, and in her entire lifetime never went more than two hundred miles from St. John's. She liked men, and had one or two "steadies" in addition to Albert Holmes, but never seemed to have strong feelings about them. I very much doubt that she ever once felt the apocalyptic frenzy of romantic love that has overwhelmed me time and again throughout my life.

Our family tended toward dead ends. Lillian had unmarried cousins, as well as an unmarried aunt. Great-aunt Anne had unmarried cousins, too, and had never married herself. The families that did get started usually ended at two or three children.

As Lillian's parents grew older, and her brothers moved away, she became the real head of the house, cooking and cleaning, managing the slender finances, nursing her parents when they became ill and feeble, making the best of their bad tempers, and, in the case of her mother, coping with senility. My grandmother Leah, a woman with enormous moral strength, true daughter of a line of merchant captains born to the quarter deck, outlived most of her contemporaries. Her powers failed slowly, and during her last two years from eighty-eight to ninety, Lillian had to tend and watch her day and night in her "second childhood," and at the same time try to run the little dairy of four to six cows. After Captain John's death in 1938, long before the deaths of her mother and aunt, Lillian began taking boarders—students at first, then, when the wartime boom began in 1941, men who came to St. John's from the northern bays to work—most of them distant family connections by marriage—Spracklins, Maidments, and so on.

She worked much harder than any of the men she served. She got up at 5:00 a.m. to start breakfasts for people who had to leave for work by 6:30. She remained on her feet until past midnight packing lunches for the next day. She cooked an immense dinner every day of her life for as many as six working men. She did their laundry and mending. And she continued to run the dairy so long as it remained possible to keep cows in an increasingly urban environment. My father, my brother and I helped with the milking, but after we had moved, and Aunt Anne was old, Lillian did all the handling of the milk and cream. She did all this while fighting off recurring attacks of migraine that did not cease until her life eased, and she began to age.

This happened when my brother married and moved back to Kalmia, and took over his share of the expenses. Meanwhile, on March 31, 1949, Newfoundland became a Canadian province, and one more member of the family became, for the first time in many years, financially independent.

Great-aunt Anne was the only one of our immediate family who went off to work in The States, as so many Newfoundlanders of her generation had done. The Boston suburb of Chelsea was settled by Newfoundland expatriots. Other members of our family had emigrated: Uncle Aubrey to Nova Scotia, Cousin Jack to the USA, where he became a building contactor, Uncle Sam to Toronto and then Brampton, where he lived into his nineties and accumulated a million dollars worth of property. But those went off to stay. Aunt Anne went off to work, intending to return.

She went first from Carbonear before the family moved to St. John's. Her journeys started in 1902, and continued until 1911. When she returned to St. John's for the last time she left $100 in a bank in Boston to take care of expenses on her next working trip. About ten years later she finally withdrew the money, now about $150, put it in a bank in St. John's and left it there "to provide a decent funeral" after her death, spending only the interest.

As far back as I can remember, Great-aunt Anne seemed to us kids like an old lady, though "lady" was hardly the word. She had the

Horwood temper, a sharp tongue, and never suffered fools gladly. When really angry she'd engage in displacement activity, like Tinbergen's gulls. Victorian ladies could not rant and rave. Instead, she'd begin to eat, furiously and savagely, attacking with venom a pile of toast, and drinking tea till her back teeth were afloat. Despite her temper, she could be very pleasant, and was both generous and kind.

Between 1911 and 1949 Aunt Anne had precious little income. In effect she worked for her keep in the house and garden. I remember her bringing turns of water before the house had plumbing, and working stacks of laundry over a scrubbing board. The air pollution from coal-burning houses in St. John's was so bad that the laundry would sometimes be stained by falling soot, and would have to be washed all over again before it dried on the outdoor line. She once fell on the ice and broke her arm. In those days no one ever salted or sanded a road. You put up with whatever was underfoot, and people sometimes wore "creepers"—little steel gadgets with blades or teeth fastened to your boots to give you a grip on the ice.

I began picking berries with Aunt Anne, a devoted berry picker, when I was seven or eight years old, and went with her for the last time when I was around fifteen and she was nearing seventy. After that, I'm afraid I had little time for maiden aunts of either generation.

Berry picking was never a chore, always a picnic. You took a lunch in a basket, and a "tin" kettle to boil tea. Shaped like a truncated cone, it would collect lots of heat through its wide-spreading bottom, even from a fire of blasty boughs, which were always to be found on the berry barrens in autumn. When the kettle boiled, you'd add the tea and boil it again for a second. This was "switchel tea" which most people drank just as it came from the kettle. We always added sugar and milk.

The boilup on the barrens helped give berry picking its flavour. We sometimes went for raspberries, which were very plentiful in some years, but blueberries could be picked by the barrel every year—it was just a matter of getting out and doing it. "Berries" meant "blueberries"[*] just as "fish" meant "cod," and the limitless crops of this wild fruit helped to carry thousands of Newfoundland families through the Great Depression.

Aunt Anne's life wasn't easy, but it ran smoothly toward the end. When she began receiving the old age pension in 1949, she was suddenly affluent after many years of penury. She not only contributed to the ordinary expenses of the house, but began buying household articles and giving gifts. She bought a new wall clock for the Salvation Army Temple in St. John's. She gave my brother Charles the violin that he continued to play until the end of his life. She was, by her standards, wealthy.

She enjoyed some years of this before she died quietly at the age of eighty-nine, having outlived her brother and his wife to become the only old person in the immediate family. I was with her when she died. She ebbed slowly, imperceptibly, toward her end, sitting at first beside the kitchen window, taking nothing but tea and a little toast, then refusing the toast, sitting later only in her bedroom, and then, during the last weeks, waking briefly, perhaps an hour at a time. Finally she lay in what seemed like a coma, but could still respond when you spoke. The last night, even the response was scarcely there. When I held her hand during the last hours, there was just the faintest answering pressure that could have been a reflex. For half a minute at a time I could not see her breathing, and could detect life only by feeling for the pulse at the side of her throat. When everything else seemed to have stopped, the heart that had pumped blood for nearly ninety years was pumping still. Her breath, drawn at incredibly long intervals, rattled gently in her throat, and the spark of life continued to glow, hour after hour through the night, as though it might glow on at this marvellously

---

* Some people called blueberries "hurts," a word their ancestors had brought from West Country England in the seventeenth century, where it was a dialect version of "whorts" or "whortleberries," a name loosely applied to almost any species of vaccinium.

low rate forever. But there simply came a time when the breath was no longer drawn, and the pulse was no longer there. It was a death of the sort for which pious Catholics used to pray. But I don't want to write it all over again. I wrote it once on pages 105 and 106 of *Tomorrow Will Be Sunday*, for Aunt Esther in the novel was in part my Aunt Anne, and there I paid her as graceful a tribute as I am likely to be able to do. She, like the others who made it possible for me to create the Newfoundland Renaissance, deserved from her country vastly more than she ever received.

A few years later, when Lillian reached the age of sixty, she qualified for Old Age Assistance. After a life of such tight budgeting, such careful management, always maintaining middle-class respectability, never sinking into poverty on even the most meagre of incomes, never seeking assistance of any kind, the federal pension with its supplement provided comfort and ease. Out of an income that so many people insisted plunged them into destitution, and in a city with the highest cost of living south of the Arctic, Lillian suddenly found herself able to open a savings account, to watch it grow, to feel secure after a life lived always on the edge.

If anyone ever deserved such a reward for having made a full contribution to the economy of the country over many years, for having served society well, for having done more than her share of the world's work while receiving less than her share of the world's wealth, Lillian was the one. Friend, companion, guide, nurse and entertainer of children for more than fifty years, she finally got to hold her first great-grand-nephew in 1980, when Samuel Noah Horwood was born to my stepdaughter Dennie and my nephew John.

Wherever I travelled over a period of forty years, Lillian followed me with letters. She was still doing it the year she died. In 1991, this eighty-nine-year-old woman was still my only regular correspondent. She had one older sister, who lived to be ninety-two, but when I reached the age of seventy in 1993 I was myself the old man of the clan.

Captain John was, of course, the great archetype of my childhood, every inch a patriarch, and my principal model for Joshua Markady in *Tomorrow Will Be Sunday*, an honour he shares with his brother-in-law, Captain Mark Burke. As I remember him he was somewhat portly, heavy-set, substantial, a man of great kindness and good humour, even though he, too, had little tolerance for fools. He wore a walrus moustache, having shaved his beard out of vanity when it turned grey, carried a walking cane, and wore the heaviest gold watch chain I can remember, stretched across his belly.

He was a great personality around St. John's. He would take his walking cane with its handle of walrus ivory intricately incised with a black design, put on his bowler hat, and walk slowly along Water Street on some minor errand, the real purpose being to pause and chat with other great personalities—lawyers, sea captains, politicians and the like, exchanging views on the state of the world and the prospects of the economy. The politicians he greeted were invariably Liberals. Captain John had voted Tory in Carbonear, but by the 1920s was a Squires Liberal, and wouldn't have been caught dead with one of the Monroe or Alderdice gang.

He often allowed me to accompany him, perhaps because I was the eldest son of an eldest son of an eldest son, and hence obviously privileged. I don't think I fidgeted while standing for what seemed like an hour at a time on Water Street listening to his incomprehensible conversations. It was an Occasion. You might be bored, but you were honoured, and it behooved you to stand at attention.

Once or twice he took me to Isaac Mercer's sail loft in downtown St. John's—a fascinating place smelling of new canvas and oakum. There men sewed sails by hand with great curved needles and leather sail palms, using linen thread. The sail loft was a kind of seaman's club, where ships' masters met to exchange gossip and discuss politics. And we viewed, but did not enter, Muir's Marble works, whose specialty, of course, was tombstones—plain slabs with names, dates and a wreath, or an angel or a cherub in the round, or a lamb lying prone on a small stone designed for the grave of an infant.

Captain John was a great man, and none knew it better than he himself. His wife, his sister, and his daughter-in-law did what they could to cut him down to size, but he survived with apparent ease. He towered above the family like a tree among shrubs.

Spending my early childhood in the house of a retired captain who loved children was a piece of great good fortune. He never tired of educating his grandsons. On the wall behind the couch where he sat (or lay for a brief nap—he spent four or five hours in bed, but napped for an additional hour or two each day) was a large map of Newfoundland. I could name its capes before I could read, and remember them yet, like a rhyme. I knew that Canada lay off to the west, Labrador and Baffin Island to the north, the United States to the south. An atlas lay on the parlour table, and on the wall of the dining room, a huge Mercator map of the world with the lands of the British Empire tinted red. In the hallway were paintings of ships in which he had sailed: I learned to name their rigs and their sails. In the years before I went to school I learned as much from Captain John as I ever learned from a teacher. He gave me not only a sense of where I lived in relation to the world, but a firm sense of my family's past, rooted in the fish trade, in the Labrador fishery, and in the mercantile town of Carbonear, whose merchant houses my grandfather spoke of as of his familiar friends.

As a child I did not know that he had ever built a ship, but I watched him build a house, do careful work with chisel and plane, just as I saw him use reference books, compute dates, and sit at a table with his books around him, writing stories of storm and shipwreck out of a crowded past—stories that gained immense importance when they were published in newspapers or magazines or books. During his latter years—he lived until I was almost fifteen—the entire household revolved around his writing.

When I compare my own childhood with the bleak infancies described by some other writers, I marvel at how culturally rich my own childhood was, despite my being born in the suburbs of a tiny colonial city among people who distrusted higher education and believed, literally, that we were all descended from Adam and Eve whom God had created six thousand years before.

Captain John's talismans included a long brass spyglass with a barrel cased in mahogany, a muzzle-loading rifle, a pocket watch of railroad accuracy, engraved with a steam locomotive to prove its authenticity, and a compass floating in its bowl of spirits. He taught us to tell the time and to read the compass before we knew our letters. When I got to grade eight, and the math teacher asked which of us could box the compass, I was the only boy in class who could do it, just as I was the only boy who knew the number of miles in a degree of latitude, or the distance from the equator to the north pole—all of it learned from an earlier generation before I went to school. The city boys in my class knew all about football and hockey, but nothing about ships. If Captain John had ever been in grade eight, every boy in his class would have known the compass, even if he couldn't remember the Rule of Three.

Captain John was strong enough, self-confident enough, to be gentle. My father told me that this Victorian patriarch had never punished a child, physically, in his life. He abhorred cruelty. As a very young man he made two trips to "the ice" hunting seals, one of them on his father's ship where he was highliner among the crew at the age of fifteen. Then he flatly refused ever to go again. Killing those helpless little creatures while they looked up at you with tears flowing from their eyes, crying for mercy, was, he said, "beneath the level of human decency." He was saying this to all-comers in the 1920s, forty years before humanitarians around the world took up the same cry.

Twenty years after Captain John's death, I began a campaign to end the atrocity of the seal hunt. In 1959 I wrote the first article ever published against the seal hunt. It appeared in the March-April issue of *Canadian Audubon*, 1960, under the title "Tragedy on the Whelping Ice." Within a year of its appearance there was a campaign among conservationists for regulation of the hunt. By 1963 *Canadian Audubon* was sending observers to the hunt, and the first regulations were in place. By 1965 there was an international clamour to stop the massacre altogether. People with great gifts for visibility and publicity had joined what was at first a one-man campaign. Later I also attacked the subject in *The Reader's Digest*, perhaps the largest mass-circulation magazine in the world. My article "Let's End the Seal Hunt for Good" was translated and published in many countries. But by then there was little need for me to go any further. Seal hunting as an industry was doomed.

It took more than a quarter of a century from the date of my first article until the sealing industry in Canada folded up. I am truly proud of the fact that this campaign was initiated in Newfoundland, by a native Newfoundlander, not, as most people suppose, by Canadian mainlanders who had "come from away." All power to Brian Davies and his ability to manipulate the media. But it was Harold Horwood, influenced by his grandfather, who initiated the attack—a truly striking example of one man's moral influence, of "ten true words spoken apart in a cave" reaching down through two generations and outward across the world to change the world's conscience. As I write this in the late 1990s, there is a determined effort by certain politicians to get mass seal hunting going again, but not much indication that it will succeed.

There was little to disturb the even flow of life in St. John's, a city that had changed its ways scarcely at all since the days of the late lamented Queen Empress. World War One had come and gone with its conscientious objectors—my father and uncle, for instance—and its white feathers and its endless succession of deaths in the mud of far-off Flanders, but that was just part of the world that had "always" existed, since the days of the Old Testament patriarchs. The railway and steamships that had arrived in the preceding century seemed like miracles; even more so the small airplanes that circled our city before heading off on death-defying attempts to reach Europe; they scarcely touched the lives of the people, who continued to live as late Victorians, looking through their windows at a world prophesied by Daniel, when many should run to and fro, and knowledge should be increased.

Wars and rumours of wars continued in far places. The earliest I remember was in China. More exciting was the rare murder that happened at home. In Corner Brook somebody named Boland and somebody named Thistle and the wife of one of them ended their triangle in a shooting, but whether the wife or the lover had shot the husband could not be proved, and it seemed that conspiracy could not be proved, either. The trial was the talk of the breakfast table; murder spiced with sex scandal. "You mark my words," Captain John predicted darkly, "they'll get off scot free." And get off they did, both of them. Later there was a hanging or two, inside the walls of the prison at Quidi Vidi. A murder might provide Captain John, who had a taste for the hideous and the bizarre, with dinner conversation; if there was nothing current he would recall some unsolved beheading that had happened on the road to Carbonear in his youth, or the time Catholics and Protestants killed each other in an election riot; lacking that he might describe an accident of special horror in which the victim was reduced "to a grease spot." Nothing of the sort was said about a hanging; the ritual killing, carried out by society against a lone victim, had little to do with guilt, punishment or revenge; it was human sacrifice, a terrible relic of a barbarous past that cast horror and gloom over us all. I'm sure Captain John approved, at least *consciously*, of hanging. But it was something that happened in the dark, beyond the pale of discussion or description. There was, indeed, such public revulsion against hanging in Newfoundland that the little country had, in effect, abolished capital punishment a full generation before it was abolished in Canada; the law remained on the books, but every killer from 1948 onwards had his sentence reduced to imprisonment.

Murders continued to be fascinating, even when there was no real danger that the murderer would end his life dancing at the end of a rope. There was a Chinese killing that had something of the mystery of a Tang war about it. There was the battle of the Hillbillies at Manuels, in which one drunken gladiator was killed. There was a ghastly incident at St. Philip's where two young men and a boy battered a middle-aged woman to death. For a society as tame as ours such scattered eruptions of violence provided the horror some of us needed. Nuclear bombs and napalm and mass-murder of civilians still hadn't entered our living rooms. We were, in fact, living the last dream of the self-improving society. We believed that torture and massacre, instituted and approved by governments, were things of the past.

Chapter 3

The first Christmas I remember was the year we had our first tree, 1927, and Christmas trees were still a novelty in Newfoundland. Most of our Christmas customs had come with our ancestors from seventeenth-century England—wassail bowls, troops of mummers, the Christmas pig raised at home for the annual feast. We had holly, of course, and windows with lighted wreaths, even the flicker of the yule log in a few big houses with large fireplaces.

Grandmother Leah always called January 6, the Twelfth Night of Shakespeare's time, Old Christmas Day, and this expression must have harked back to the time of the reform of the calendar under Pope Gregory XIII in the sixteenth century (a reform adopted only later in England). In my grandmother's youth January 6 was indeed Christmas Day as reckoned by the pre-Gregorian calendar.

My parents, Russellites with strong views about pagan customs, would not have approved of a Christmas tree, Norse symbol from Germany as it was. My father told me that the tree symbolized the resurrection of the yule log, which had been cut down and burned, and was part of a pagan vegetation cult. But Captain John had decided we should have the tree, and the two aunts, Lillian and Anne, had concurred.

That tree, as I recall it, was hundreds of feet tall, towering to heaven, a blue-green spruce, bluer, I believe, than anything that grew before or since, and far spicier, Its resin, like crystal jewels on the tips of its twigs, filled our whole house with spicy perfume. At the centre of the parlour it rose, a glittering cone between the varnished pitch pine of the ceiling and the varnished maple of the floor. The tree did not live in the midst of our family, in the kitchen. Instead, we paid it visits, like pilgrims to a shrine.

Great-aunt Anne knew by instinct how to turn a tree into the first magic object of a child's world, a ladder joining heaven to the abyss, a tree of life bearing the fruits of paradise. Some of those fruits were pure objects of vision, but others were perfectly edible, for besides the glittering tinsel and the silvered glass, blown into universes that a small child could hold in his hands, the tree was hung with jewelled candies, with clusters of foil-wrapped chocolates, with striped peppermint canes, and with bunches of real grapes, red and purple and green, all tied to its twigs with the brittle Christmas string that even a small child's fingers could break. As my brother and I gathered our private harvests from the tree, its lower branches would grow somewhat denuded, but at night it had a strange power of regeneration, and bore new crops of heavenly offerings at dawn.

The fruits of that tree had not been made shoddy by daily abundance. The exotic magic of a gum drop, glowing like a ruby with trapped light, and encrusted with sequins of sugar crystals, has by now simply vanished from the earth. In my childhood it came, like other edible jewels, out of the Arabian Nights on silver trays borne by genii.

Most of the gifts that appeared under that tree on Christmas morning have vanished in the corrosive flux of time. Perhaps there were prosaic things like mittens and teddy bears and wind-up metal toys; I don't know; they are lost. But among them was one that remains in memory almost as fresh as the tree itself. It was a boat—a toy sloop with a red wooden hull and a white sail, real rigging that you could adjust, and a deep keel so that in a light breeze on a small pond it would come alive with a will and a purpose all its own.

It was an inspired gift that, I learned later, had been chosen by the same great aunt who knew how to convert a tree into an object of myth and magic. It has sailed ever since through the technicolour seascapes of my imagination. Twenty years after it was laid away in some box of broken toys it became the beautiful ocean-going sloop that I owned and sailed to the fabulous land of Labrador. It is also the mighty ship that sails and rustles behind the world in the cosmic dreamscapes of my night visions, and will live with me until I close my eyes for the last time.

My brother and I were taken about the streets by our Aunt Lillian to see the windows hung with wreaths and candles. There was crusted snow on the hills, and we went sliding with the new coaster sleds that had appeared, I suppose, beneath the tree. One of the adults always came along, enjoying the breathtaking downhill plunge with us.

At evening there was much singing around the piano, with a visiting aunt to sing alto, an uncle to sing tenor, my father contributing a solid bass, while the rest of us made shift to hold the soprano line in such carols as "It Came upon a Midnight Clear" and "Joy to the World." But our favourite was a ballad that Captain John remembered from his youth: "While Shepherds Watched Their Flocks by Night"—a straightforward account of the Bethlehem story in song and verse.

But the transporting events of that first Christmas were not confined to visits to a magic parlour. In the humble and familiar world of the kitchen there was music and pageantry and mystery, too. For the night after Christmas the mummers arrived! That night and every night for the remaining ten days of Christmas they came tapping or scratching on our door, creatures no child could ever forget, arrayed in fearsome masks or ghost-like sheets, costumed in table cloths or lace curtains, some of the men in petticoats and bonnets, women in fishing boots and overalls, speaking in squeaky voices with indrawn breath, singing off-key. They played mouth organs, rarely a concertina or fiddle. Part of the game was to "unmask" the visitors by guessing who they were.

Great-aunt Anne, making shift to be pious in her old age, was dead set against the "jannies" as she called them. It was the devil's foolery, she declared, and if she had her way they wouldn't be allowed into the house at all. But my father told me with a wink that she had dressed up as a "jannie" herself when she was young, and had gone the rounds of Carbonear with the most boisterous of the lot. One Christmas, disguised as a man in a Sunday suit, she had been set upon by her own dog, who failed to discover his mistake before he had ripped a long strip from her expensive borrowed trousers. After that she joined the Salvation Army and swore off mummering for life.

More fearsome than any mummer was the hobby horse—looking more like a dragon than a horse, with its long wooden jaws hinged and set with nails for teeth, worked by strings from inside, and snapping together with an awesome crack while the hobby horse went wriggling around the outside of the house trying to get in. No one that I heard of ever let a hobby horse indoors, and the mummers who entertained us in our kitchens and ate our Christmas fare took cake and wine out "to feed the horse" as they put it.

The mummers had gone in procession on real horses in my grandfather's youth, and they had a "king of the mummers" in charge of their parades. Captain John told us how they used to perform "the mummers' play" at Government House for the entertainment of the English admirals who used to rule our land. Then they would repeat the play at some of the other big houses where the merchants lived. The play was said to be ancient. In it St. George fought the Turkish Knight and various other champions, and everyone who got killed was brought back to life again by the magic potions of a powerful mummer called "the doctor."

The Salvation Army provided a sort of sacred counterpoint to the mummers' profane entertainments. Their brass bands toured from door to door playing carols. But instead of giving them wine and cake, like mummers, you dropped coins into little boxes that they carried. They had cornets and trombones and tenor horns and a big tuba and a brass drum, so you could hear them clear across town. Sometimes the whole band would be invited in for dinner, and the table would almost bend under cold pork and goose meat and cookies and cake and fruit syrup.

On such occasions the jugs of blueberry wine stayed discreetly in the closet under the stairs, for all Salvationists had "taken the pledge."

My grandmother was the one who made the wine—dark and heavy and sweet, like port, though not quite as strong. But because it was "natural" wine from fruit that you gathered yourself in the hills behind town, it was permissable for special occasions like weddings and Christmas, even in strict temperance houses like ours. More than one guest went weaving home after drinking generous tumblers of Grandmother Leah's blueberry wine, blessing the kind of temperance she believed in. Even small children might be allowed a sip—not much more—in glasses about the size of thimbles. Sadly, the time came when Mr. Butt, he who worked with Captain John, drank so much blueberry wine that he became obviously tipsy. Grandmother Leah was horrified. She had never guessed what devil's poison she was brewing. She took her cask of blueberry wine, poured it out on the ground, and never brewed another drop as long as she lived.

Though wine was *the* Christmas drink, homemade spruce beer, or even moonshine, was plentiful in some houses. Not long ago I was in an outport kitchen where eighty-two bottles of home-made rum were ranged around the wainscotting, a sort of public announcement that no guest would go dry in *this* house. Moonshining was a little bit against the law, of course, even in Newfoundland, but was so widespread that not much effort was made to stop it unless the stuff was being made for sale.

Amongst Christmas visitors, those who came without masks were almost as impressive as the mummers. There was Cousin Stewart, spending a Christmas at home between voyages, with his aura of worldliness and his fruit-cured rum, his enormous seaman's guernsey, and his face round and red like the sun rising above a hill. He brought exotic confections wrapped in multicoloured tinsel, and out of the tinsel he made little boots for our tabby cat, a different colour for each foot. The cat, unaccountably, seemed less than pleased with this attention; after taking a few comical steps she sat down and pulled off the bootees with her teeth, then stalked away indignantly to her place behind the kitchen range.

Our Great-uncle Sam, Grandfather's brother, was there too, home with a full load of fish from Labrador. As he walked, he rolled from side to side, as though the deck were pitching under him, and when he told about his voyage, his voice rattled the window panes as though he were still shouting commands above the booming of the surf while the trap crews worked their nets along a stormy shore. Skipper Sam brought gifts of red-gold salmon cured in his own smokehouse over smouldering turf and bark and blackberry shrubs. He also brought amber bakeapples, which foreigners called cloudberries, ripened on the misty Labrador peat bogs and prized by Newfoundlanders as the most beloved of all the fruits of the earth.

And then there was Great-aunt Kiziah McCarthy ("Aunt Kizz"), a woman as monumental as her name, owner of a large house right on the waterfront at Carbonear, but spending much of her second widowhood visiting relatives in St. John's. Aunt Kizz had a touch of high blood pressure and a slight tremble in hands and head, which somehow seemed only to add to her overpowering dignity. I remember her enthroned on our kitchen settle, behind the end of the big table, in conversation about matters that did not interest me. Her house in Carbonear was always open to us, its spare bedrooms piled high with feather beds for our use any time we went travelling to the ancestral home. Aunt Kizz had been ordered by her doctor not to eat salt, and liked to describe herself as suffering from "salt diabetes," a condition that must have been common in Newfoundland, where salt was used not only to preserve beef, pork and all kinds of fish, but was poured into the cooking pots, and finally sprinkled over the food as condiment. Aunt Kizz, by her first marriage, was sister-in-law to Grandmother Leah, and had a son named Willis Burke who also came visiting.

Our Great-aunt Sally, Captain John's cousin, sister to the people who had founded the Horwood Lumber Company, moved through that world of tribal elders, a woman unimaginably old, with a trumpet-shaped hearing aid, a lorgnette on a ribbon, and a dress of black satin frosted with glass beads that caught the lights and threw them back in flashes of many-coloured fire.

There must have been children, too, at least occasionally, but I have forgotten them. It is not the companions, the playmates, that one recalls from the myth-making days of earliest youth, but the gods that peopled the slopes of one's private Olympus. It is still a matter of some wonder to me that those remote beings, concerned with vast affairs of trade and commerce, conquerors of the sea and companions of the storm, should have thought at all about the trifles that connect childhood to the land of vision—the smell of spruce gum, the glitter of silvered glass, the glowing colours of paper and tinsel. Yet, somehow, a being as Olympian as Captain John reached across the gap and knew the importance of such trifles and provided them.

He was quite capable, just the same, of destroying playthings that annoyed him. Andrew's employer, Albert Hickman, had made me a present shortly after I was born of a large "mama" doll, under the impression that I was a girl. This doll, named after Hickman's daughter Joan, had a very realistic cry when tilted at the proper angle. One day Captain John came into the house, settled majestically into an easy chair, then shot to his feet as he felt beneath him a soft bundle that screamed "Mama!"

"By the water's flame!" he shouted, grabbing the doll that he had mistaken for a baby. He pulled the cover off the kitchen range and stuffed Joan into the firebox. Grandmother Leah, the only witness to the incident, rushed to Joan's rescue—but too late. Her celluloid face was melted; her body was in flames. Grandmother, nonetheless, dipped Joan into the nearest pail of water, and tried to salvage the remains. For many years we all thought that somebody had stolen Joan from the front veranda. Then, after Captain John's death, my grandmother fetched out the doll's innards from a bedroom closet, and told us what had happened. The disembodied voicebox could still cry "Mama!" as convincingly as ever.

I believe the images of that first remembered Christmas when I was four years old coloured my later career as an imaginative writer, helped to shape my private mythology, and supplied some of my recurring symbols. Consciously or otherwise I have used crystal globes as images of the universe, and trees as symbols of life and strength and immortality. The imprinting that a child undergoes from such joyous experiences can enrich his entire life. If the experience grows out of folklore and custom, so much the better: the child is then enriched with the accumulated symbolism of the race.

I have long believed that Jung's "collective unconscious" might be a social phenomenon such as this, rather than the metaphysical miracle that he seems to have supposed. The more of Jung's essays that I read, the more settled the belief becomes. I suspect that archetypes are fixed in our unconscious in childhood, transmitted by custom and story, by lullaby and fairy tale, to reappear in visions and dreams much the same the world over regardless of cultural variations because the archetypes tend to be cross-cultural constants, elements of folklore everywhere. I do not believe that we should postulate difficult explanations where simple ones will serve us better, or create magical mystery scenarios where rational ones will suffice. This does not mean that I reject magic and mystery; on the contrary, I believe that magic and mystery are the very fabric of what I am talking about, and that the birth of magic comes about in each of us in the way I have described.

Christmas Day was not a holy day in our private calendar; we all knew that it was really a pagan festival associated with the winter solstice, not the anniversary of the birth of Christ. New Year's Eve, oddly enough, came closer to being a Protestant holy day. None of us went to parties on New Year's Eve, but many went to church, and those who did not held an abbreviated Watch Night Service at home.

Watch Night Services were celebrated by Methodists, the Salvation Army, and even the Russellites, sometimes, I'm not sure who else. They started around 11:00 pm and ended around 12:30 or 1:00 am on New Year's Day. They were the occasion for readings or sermons about the Arrow of Time, and God's provision for the earthly welfare of his saints. Special hymns were sung. A Watch Night hymn that my grandfather loved (though he never attended a service in my lifetime) went like this:

> Come, let us anew
> Our journey pursue,
> Roll around with the years,
> Roll around with the years,
> And never stand still
> Till the Master appears.
>
> Our life like a dream.
> Our time like a stream,
> Glide swiftly away...

It had a fine majestic melody, and I recall singing it on one occasion with my grandfather over the telephone after we had moved out of his house. Another hymn sung at Watch Night was "O God our help in ages past." It had some tolerably good passages:

> Time like an ever-rolling stream
> Bears all its sons away;
> They fly forgotten, as a dream
> Dies at the opening day.

Many years later I realized that this hymn was a rather poor attempt to paraphrase one of the most splendid of the psalms:

> Lord Thou hast been our dwelling place in all generations
> Before the mountains were brought forth
> Or ever Thou hadst formed
> The earth and the world,

> Even from everlasting to everlasting
> Thou art God.
> Thou turnest men to destruction
> And sayest, Return ye children of men;
> For a thousand years in Thy sight
> Are but as yesterday when it is past,
> And as a watch in the night.

When I was around twenty years old I wrote a recitative on this passage, which has a marvellous natural rhythm. I suppose writers of church music must often have "set" the words, though I have never heard any setting except my own.

At some time in my early childhood, long before I went to school, there was a decision that I should be allowed to stay up "to see the new year in" as all the elder members of the household did. Since at that time I was being sent to bed every evening before six o'clock, staying up till midnight was an incredible change, and it is not surprising that by eight-thirty I was pestering my elders to know how much longer it would be to midnight. I groggily recalled Aunt Lillian telling me that it was now nine o'clock, an hour that seemed to me rather like halfway to the moon. Then I knew no more until she shook me awake in time to hear the thunder of distant guns and the howling of sirens from ships moored in the harbour. In the midst of it all there was a tremendous explosion not far from our window, and someone said that it was Paddy Lewis letting off both barrels of his twelve-gauge shotgun.

Then I fell asleep and was chased by bears, or crocodiles, or foxes, or some other bloodthirsty animal, as happened night after night when I was a small child. The Freudians say such dreams are caused by fear of your father, that the bull, or whatever it is that's chasing you, is really your old man. I doubt that this could have been true in my case; Andrew was not a very frightening parent. Much more likely, I think, the dreams were caused by the talk around the dinner table of the danger of bears eating children, and of the frightful risk posed by domestic bulls, and even by cows and horses. According to most of the adults in our household, just about everything on four legs was out to get you if it could.

Many adults seem to have gone out of their way to instill fear in small children, to communicate their own fears, to create new ones. Thus Captain John, who had an irrational fear of dogs, probably acquired on Labrador, taught us to be afraid of dogs. Grandmother Leah taught us to be afraid of insects. They all combined to make us afraid of cows, probably because they really feared that we might be accidentally trampled or caught by a horn. For some reason or other, probably stirred by their own superstitions, they taught us to be afraid of the dark.

None of these fears is "natural" or instinctive. Perhaps a fear of snakes is instinctive in many people, but a fear of insects, dogs, cattle and horses most certainly is not. And fear of the dark is not instinctive, either. Many people believe it is because many children are still taught in infancy to be afraid of the dark. My own children have never had the slightest trace of any of those fears. They have always liked the dark, and felt safe in it. The only irrational fear that might have been communicated to them in early childhood was their mother's fear of snakes; somehow, they escaped it. Even being stung repeatedly by bees and wasps did not create an irrational fear in either of them—it just taught them to be careful. Neither of them ever had dreams of being chased by animals or monsters.

What lifelong difference this might make I can't imagine; at least, I should think, it ought to free them from the pervading sense of insecurity that follows so many people throughout their lives. At the same time, they grew up, from the age of six or seven, with the knowledge that the Americans could, and perhaps would, destroy the whole world with hardly a moment's notice. What effect *that* might have I can't guess either.

January 1 was what my father called "Gentlemen's Visiting Day" when many of the VIPs from the governor to the big merchants held open house and welcomed all comers. I don't remember Captain John walking out on Gentlemen's Visiting Day, but Andrew made a great ceremony of it, putting on his pearl-grey spats and his white silk scarf, with his navy blue suit, his walking cane, and his soft felt hat. He also wore a pocket watch with a modest gold chain.

Some time after moving to St. John's from Carbonear, my father came into contact with the Berean Bible Students founded by Charles Taze Russell. My mother was also a member of this congregation before she married, and like her husband remained with it all her life. They became rather more liberal and tolerant as they grew older, but, except for a somewhat expanded view of the universe, following the discovery that the nebulae were in fact "other universes" than ours, they hardly absorbed a new idea during my lifetime.

My parents, it seems to me, didn't have a great social life. Their "meetings" with the "class" of Russellites on Sunday afternoons and evenings and at least one night a week largely took the place of other social activities, and gave my father a sense of achievement, for no matter how small the "little flock" might be, he was always its chief elder, its ablest speaker, and the one most deeply steeped in the eschatological interpretations of the Bible propounded by Russell, who was himself a successor to Miller and the Millerites.

When the Jehovah's Witnesses began to evolve out of the Russellites, and to stray further and further from the corpus of pure truth that Russell had enshrined in his six volumes of *Studies in the Scriptures,* there was a great crisis, and the little flock at St. John's split in two, one faction following my father back to the original Russellite teachings, eventually joining the Dawn Bible Students, while the other faction became more and more militant Jehovah's Witnesses, on their way to building their Kingdom Halls across the land, refusing blood transfusions, and consigning to the Second Death those who rejected their clear light.

It was a strange intellectual climate for a small child, but one that encouraged some kind of critical examination of life and belief. I have always believed that my father had a critical and enquiring mind up to the age of twenty or so, and that there, somehow or other, he stopped, retreated into what was for him a kind of orthodoxy, and held to it for the rest of his life. Religion was a very big thing in our immediate family. Andrew and Vina were not just "religious" in the ordinary sense. Their lives positively revolved around their beliefs and rituals, and the gathering in of the "wheat" for the Lord's Harvest.

Our family history has been one of following smaller and smaller schisms on the fragmented edge of radical protestantism. The Horwoods who came out to Virginia and Newfoundland in the seventeenth century must have been followers of the Church of England, like their patrons in Great Britain. But they tended toward radicalism even in early colonial times. According to family tradition received through my grandfather, one of them was hanged for treason in England, where he had gone with a petition for redress of grievances by the colonists. And another, Great-uncle Noah Horwood, was hanged for piracy in Jamaica. They might have fought their private enemies, but not one of them ever fought for the state (for King and country, as they used to say). One of my proudest boasts is that no member of my family, as far back as it can be traced, has ever fought in a war.

My father's and mother's people converted to Wesleyism, perhaps in the 1760s, when Lawrence Coughlan was preaching and setting up religious communities and the first schools at Harbour Grace, Carbonear, and other east coast outports. My grandmother's people, the Burkes, probably became Wesleyans at the same time, though they were never radical like the Horwoods. Coughlan's great success was due in part to his having walked into a religious desert, at a time when no church building existed in Conception Bay, and services were held just occasionally by visiting ministers from St. John's. In the late nineteenth century the Salvation Army arrived, and early in the twentieth, the Russellites and the Pentecostals.

Captain John remained aloof from it all. He liked to sing hymns, but was not a religious man. Younger members of the family, from

Captain John's kid sister Anne all down the line, "joined the Army." Andrew and his brother Sam played in the band. Lillian taught at a Salvation Army school and Sunday school. Millie, her elder sister, wore the uniform throughout her life.

My father was what I would call a "liberal fundamentalist." He believed the Bible was God's Word to mankind, but interpreted a great deal of it symbolically. He did not believe that the world was made in six days or that every living creature except those on the ark had died in Noah's flood, or a host of other absurdities to which radical fundamentalists everywhere adhere, but many absurdities remained: the belief, for example, that every human being who had ever lived (except for a handful of Christian saints translated to heaven) would be physically resurrected and remain on earth for a thousand years until the Last Judgement, and, if they escaped the Second Death, thenceforth forever.

In my late teens I had a brief fling with Christianity, and joined my father's congregation, but soon began questioning its doctrines. By the age of twenty-one, had I wished to remain a Christian, I would have had to found my own sect. Instead, over the next few years, I began to view all Christian doctrine as absurd. Still later in life I came to regard the whole Christian movement from the second or third century onwards as the greatest cultural and intellectual disaster that had ever befallen the civilized world.

My teenage experiences with Christianity, and my father's preaching, had lasting effects. I still accept the doctrines of pacifism, the ethics of the Sermon on the Mount, and have a lifelong love for the Hebrew prophets. But perhaps the most lasting effect was from the mystical experience that came to me first when I was a sixteen-year-old Christian. There was, of course, no room for a mystic among the Russellites, or indeed in any of the fundamentalist sects, but I didn't know that at the time. Nor did I know that the human mystic is a comparatively rare animal, that of the millions of church-going Christians hardly a handful ever experience the shattering event of having the heavens open and the whole universe flood into them. It happened to me, then, and later, after I had abandoned Christianity. At the time I thought of it as a "gratuitous grace" but I have come to believe since that a long period of meditation and self-discipline actually led up to it. Once you have experienced the mystical vision, it is relatively easy to experience it again, by other routes—as happened to me with Zen Buddhism, and finally with LSD.

As a child I hated the "meetings." My father's "talks"—they were never called "sermons"—were delivered extemporaneously, with a few jotted notes and Bible texts. But by the time I was six or seven I had heard every argument he would ever advance, listened to every theme in his theology, knew it all by heart. Many of the oft-quoted passages were very beautiful, for they concerned mainly the "times of restitution...which God hath spoken by the mouth of all his holy prophets since the world began." Those passages, written by Jews in exile yearning for the restoration of Zion, were exceptional literary texts, whether applied to their original intention or misapplied to a coming Millennium when the weaned child should put his hand on the cockatrice's den, and every householder in the world should sit under his own vine and fig tree.

I still don't know what animal the Elizabethans were talking about when they referred to a cockatrice, but it sounds like something with a poisonous bite.

Endless repetition made the "meetings" a bore. I didn't realize until much later that my father was talking to people with a far lower level of intelligence than mine, and without my knack for remembering every beautiful combination of words I had ever heard. Later on, that knack made me the envy of the brightest kids in school when we had to commit poems to memory, something I could usually do at a single reading. I still have thousands of lines of good and bad poetry filed away in my memory, along with the indelible prophets. Both had a profound effect on my prose, and my use of imagery.

I learned to read mainly in the "study" classes where we sat in a circle and read through the six volumes of *Studies in the Scriptures*. Russell's intention had been to write seven of them, thus fulfilling the prophecy of the sounding of the seven trumpets in the Book of Revelation, but he didn't live to complete the set. The seventh—*The Finished Mystery*—was put together after his death, and though it incorporated many of his ideas, it was not canonical among true Russellites.

Unlike the Biblical texts and the poetry, Mr. Russell's prose had no effect on me that I can recall other than teaching me to read. I remember the outline of his Divine Plan of the Ages, of course, but I have trouble remembering even the titles of some of his books. Bible students were said to be "in the truth." I'm willing to bet that not one of them, in the whole history of the sect, was aware that this phrase came down from Akhenaton, the prophet-king of Egypt. Everyone else was "in the world," but not thereby lost or damned. The world, too, would be redeemed in the Times of Restitution, while the handful "in the truth" would go to heaven, there to be rulers with Christ over the universe.

The meetings did something for my musical education, too. By six or seven I could pick out hymn tunes on the piano, and by ten I could add chord progressions by ear. I could soon read simple music, and by the age of fifteen could play just about every hymn ever written, hundreds of them from memory, so I often played the organ in religious services. Though I played more complex music later, and as an adult began to develop some musical taste, I still like to play hymns on the Victorian pump organ in my own house. Listening with delight to Bach and Palestrina and Prokofiev, as I do now, may well have had its foundation in the simple rhythms and four-part harmonies of the hymn book.

What else? The deep moral sense—the feeling that we should do something worthwhile with our lives—may have come to me from those "consecrated" Christians among whom I moved as a child. It is a feeling I've never outgrown or given up, though I soon outgrew the rules and taboos that went with it.

My father's congregation was always very small, about ten to twenty souls, never more than thirty. The concept of such a small group being "in the truth" and everybody else hopelessly in error may well have stimulated my critical sense and developed my lifelong will to be an outsider. I've always felt that majorities were nearly certain to be wrong, that error is enthroned as a matter of course, and that if there is any hope for the world it lies with a small minority of the ethical and intellectual elite.

From my father, and even more, perhaps, from my grandfather, I must have conceived the belief that I had something to say to which the world ought to listen. It requires, I suppose, an unusual strength of ego to believe this, to think of yourself not just as an artist, but as a leader in the rarefied field of human wisdom. More than just ego, it requires a sense of calling, a sense of being dedicated to something well beyond the common human condition. And such a sense may well have come out of a childhood like mine, flanked by a father who believed he had been chosen to be co-ruler of the universe with the Risen Christ, and a grandfather who ignored his son's religious maunderings but who, in the words of my friend Irving Fogwill, believed he could show God a few tricks.

Chapter 4

On the corner of St. Clare and Mt. Pleasant Avenues stood the "Tin House," a large square building covered in sheet metal, the only thing of its kind we'd ever seen. Between the tin house and our kitchen window was a muddy intermittent pond that dried up in summer, and, at the edge of the narrow dirt road, a boulder standing out of the earth, just right for small boys to climb upon. These were the only natural features of note in the immediate vicinity. You could skate on the pond in winter, and sled down Mt. Pleasant Avenue. All this came to an end a few years later when the road was asphalted, the boulder removed, the pond covered with concrete, and the tin house with conventional siding.

We skated on the roads in winter and rode tricycles there in summer. We scratched squares in the dust and played hopscotch, which was mainly a girls' game, but one that boys often played as well. We scooped out "mots" in the ground, shallow round holes, and tossed marbles or "alleys" at them, shooting in the ones that missed, last finisher taking the works. This was the only marble game that I saw played at home or at school. The American game with the circle and marbles shot against one another hadn't yet arrived. Most marbles were baked spheres of pottery clay in various colours. "Alleys" (the word must have been a corruption of "aggies," itself a corruption of "agates") were made of glass with magic coloured insertions, spirals of blue and red and yellow wound about a central core, far more beautiful than the cheap mottled glass ones that came later. Any alley was worth ten marbles, and there were a few giant alleys worth ten of the small ones. Large ball bearings of stainless steel sometimes found their way into alley collections, too. A bag with a drawstring was the only way to carry them; the larger your collection, the higher your status; the useless spheres were as jealously guarded as a miser's gold. The season for marbles was short, beginning after the snow went, and ending in May.

Chasing hoops went on all summer. You used a short stick to roll and steer your hoop, which might be a round band of sheet steel from a wooden drum, or a much grander iron hoop from a cartwheel, a treasure owned by very few. Perhaps hoops were sometimes borrowed from the women who used them to help balance the "turns" of water that they carried, two buckets at a time, from the public cisterns.

By 1928 Andrew owned a car. His first was an Overland convertible with a glass windscreen and side windows of celluloid that you attached with studs in bad weather. A drive with the family around Twenty Mile Pond (later called Windsor Lake) was one of his favourites. A visit to Topsail Beach was another. There we would wade in the icy water, and skip flat stones on the surface if it was calm enough. Sometimes he'd rent a skiff for a twenty-cent piece and take us rowing. Two or three times a year we'd make the enormous journey to Carbonear, nearly a day's drive, what with stops to change flat tires and a boilup for lunch on the Brigus Barrens.

The road in those days followed the shoreline, dipping down into the Irish settlements of Holyrood and Harbour Main and Colliers, where the boys ran about barefoot and the goats wore wooden yokes to keep them from squeezing through the fences into the cabbage patches. At Avondale a little river that came pouring down between the rugged hills was led through a flume to turn the huge wooden wheel of a sawmill, the last water-powered mill on the shore of Conception Bay, and the only one we ever saw as children.

On the Brigus Barrens, just above Turk's Gut, was a small lake with a grassy bank, and just across the road a sheer cliff with a rocking stone sitting on its brink. Here we invariably stopped for lunch, and

Andrew built a fire in a circle of stones, using blasty boughs and dry sticks which we gathered from the woods. After we'd eaten, while the adults cleaned up and repacked, Charlie and I would climb the ledges to the rocking stone, and try vainly to push it over the edge. Then we'd drive on past Clarke's Beach and Bareneed (a corruption of Barren Head, Andrew told us), to the Tilton Barrens and the descent to River Head, Harbour Grace, where the Orangemen and the Irish had fought with guns in our grandfather's time. Finally we'd cross Saddle Hill to Carbonear, and make the rounds of the relatives' houses.

Between Holyrood and Carbonear the bay was well supplied with harbours and well populated with people and ships. This short stretch included many famous ports—Harbour Grace, Spaniard's Bay, Bay Roberts, Cupids and Brigus—populated with mariners and fishermen, Arctic explorers and sealing captains, some of them famous, and some of them prosperous.

Northward from Carbonear the land and the people changed completely. Here there were no good harbours until you reached distant Bay de Verde; consequently, there were no ships, just small fishing boats, and the people were correspondingly poor. I'm afraid the snobbish Carbonearmen regarded the North Shore people as hillbillies, inferior and amusing. We were never taken, as kids, to the North Shore, but I went there often as an adult, and met people full of warmth and kindness well beyond what you would expect in purse-proud Carbonear.

Just once we drove over the nearly impassable road from Carbonear to Heart's Content where Grandmother Leah had walked, as a young woman, to see the enormous steamship *Great Eastern* land the first transatlantic cable linking Europe with North America. At Heart's Content we were able to buy gasoline from what must have been the only service station on the southeast shore of Trinity Bay at that time. The red liquid was pumped up by hand from an underground tank to fill an overhead glass cistern, and then fed by gravity into the car.

From those long drives we sometimes returned to St. John's at night, when we might see the full moon rise over the sea stretching eastward from Clarke's Beach or Harbour Main. We often brought back to the city red slabs of smoked salmon or bags of capelin cured in backyard smokehouses.

One of the places we always visited in Carbonear was Aunt Kiziah McCarthy's. Another was the big house on the hill above Carbonear owned by Captain Windsor, a first cousin of Captain John's. There were certain unfamiliar traditions in that house. It was the first place I ever tasted goat's milk, or bread made with hops, which grew on a trellis in front of the Windsor veranda. The house was most interesting, though, for the many souvenirs that Captain Windsor had brought home from his foreign voyages: tiny china figurines, stuffed flying fish, carved gourds from the West Indies. For some reason, the men of our own family had never bothered with such trifles.

Almost as interesting as the visits to Carbonear were the visits we made with our father to the St. John's waterfront. Though we no longer lived at the landwash, as our people had done for uncounted generations, we still had a nodding acquaintance with the sea. At the harbour, as at Mundy Pond, we sometimes saw boys swimming in the nude. Southside boys would swim right across to the docks on the north side and climb out, panting, but after a short rest they would have no choice, being naked, but to dive back in and swim home.

Andrew once took us to see a great whale that had been towed into the harbour by a ship. It was big beyond all imagining: a child could barely climb to its back by way of its tail, but once aloft you were on a surface like a gentle hill, firm and smooth, and you could dare your brother to race you all the way to the head that rose like a bluff cape from the oily water. Another time there were live seals swimming and diving inside a wire enclosure, and catching herring when you tossed one into the air.

But above all, at the harbour were the ships, white ships, black ships, rising and falling at the piers like horses champing to be off and running. But those were creatures with very neat and compact living quarters inside, like miniature houses. They had come from Moreton's Harbour and Sagona and Isle aux Morts, places that were only names to us, but names often spoken by our elders, filled with a curious romance, impelling us to wander, to seek far-off places. And to us wandering meant only one thing—standing on the deck of a ship as it rose and fell in the sea, its bows hissing with foam.

Our actual seafaring in preschool days was limited to trapboat voyages from the Southside premises owned by John Strong, or rowboat trips on Conception Bay, but most of our fluvial excursions were on the pond at Bowring Park, where we learned to handle oars, to tie up and cast off, and to approach the dock without smashing into it bow-first.

Moored "in the stream" on anchors in mid-harbour we'd see big vessels that had come to St. John's from foreign ports, sometimes flying the "yellow jack," a quarantine flag which meant that they had not yet been given a "clean bill of health" by the medical officer. Captain John explained the meaning of the square yellow flag and told horrifying tales of pest ships in which whole crews had died in the harbour.

"One time a ship from England went in to Norway," he told us. "and she had the Black Death on board. So they made her stand at anchor for a month while everyone on her from the captain to the cabin boy died a frightful death, with black swellings that would burst and run with pus until they rotted right away where they lay on the deck, roaring with pain. Then they towed the ship off her moorings and burned her, right to the water's edge, with all the corpses still on board. But some of the rats managed to swim ashore, and they took the Black Death with them, and thousands of Norwegians died that summer."

The ships, when they didn't smell of salt fish, smelled of new manilla rope and tar, sometimes of bilgewater, of rot, of decay, but often, too, of fresh paint, and always there was a pervasive scent of the sea, like a beach at low tide. They were inanimate creatures, of course, but almost an organic world of their own, almost living things, evolved as much out of the sea as out of the human imagination, the product of man married to the ocean, with the special voices and personalities of that magical hybridizing. They were supple, responsive creations, able to live with the world, even with the world of wind and storm and crashing comber, slipping successfully through the sea's lanes and valleys, never confronting it in a brutal battle of wills, but finding the way to travel with the flow.

This was the essence of a ship, as every sailor knew instinctively. And we who were born into families of sailors knew it without ever being told; there were many things about ships and the sea that we never needed to learn; they were as much a part of us as the soil was part of the European peasants who settled in Ontario and Quebec. When at the age of twenty-six I came to the point of owning and sailing my own ship, it was one of the supreme experiences of my life—not the fulfilment of a childhood ambition but the fulfilment of a family destiny. Even when I sailed it through a savage storm on the coast of Labrador I felt completely at home, completely right. This was where I belonged. I've been at sea in a number of bad storms without any sense of terror.

In childhood, of course, none of this was conscious. We were simply drawn to ships like calves to the udder, and much later, when we began handling them, we seemed to know how to do it without being taught. Just visiting them in childhood, wandering through cabin and fo'castle and galley, and feeling them move under our feet, was enough.

Unlike outport boys we never went "copying" over the sea ice, jumping from pan to pan, or floating around on ice rafts, but we did walk out on the ice of Conception Bay once or twice when it was tight to the shore, and one afternoon when the arctic floes had packed tightly into St. John's harbour we walked as far as the Chain Rock at the Narrows and felt the ice heaving gently under our feet as the swells pressed in from the open sea.

Winter was not, however, a time of much joy. For one thing, I was always sick. A cold would start in my head, progress down to my throat, thence to my chest, and I'd be coughing for four or five weeks. A few days after the cough finally cleared up, the whole cycle of misery would start over again. Every cold I ever caught wound up on my chest until I became a man and learned how to deal with a cold in its early stages.

Fifty years after my brother and I went ice hiking, my children, Andrew and Leah, were floating about on ice pans on the shore of Annapolis Basin, where tide and spray and frost conspire to produce them locally. So it isn't a matter of tradition, just something children will do if they get the chance. No girl in our childhood would have played on the ice. It was reserved for boys, who were often forbidden to do it, but who did it anyway, in accordance with sex roles laid down in infancy. Had Captain John found a granddaughter playing on the ice he would have scolded her and repeated the old rhyme:

> A whistling woman and a crowing hen
> Is good for neither God nor men.

Girls cooked, embroidered, cleaned house, weeded gardens, played "shop" or "school" and dressed dolls. Boys got to do all the interesting, adventurous and dangerous things, and a certain number of them in every generation died in accidents, mostly by drowning. Among the boys I knew one was drowned, one was killed by a car, and one was killed accidentally by a rifle bullet. In our house they would never have dreamed of allowing us to handle guns, but many boys began using them, at least shooting at targets, by the age of eight or ten.

I was seven years old when we went on our first real voyage, all the way to Canada on the *S.S Nova Scotia*, and back on the *S.S. Fort George*, ships of the Furness Withy and Red Cross Lines, then operating between Liverpool, St. John's, Halifax and Boston. We went with Vina to spend the summer at her father's farm near Gagetown, New Brunswick. On the outward trip we also had our first real train journey—from Halifax through Truro and Moncton to Saint John, and then on another train up the Saint John River Valley to Gagetown.

The part I remember best was the trip from Saint John to Gagetown, incredibly slow, on a train that stopped at the back of practically every farm to collect pails of milk for a dairy. That train crawled right through the back of my grandfather's farm, and as I remember it took most of the day to cover the seventy-five miles between Saint John and Fredericton.

That was our first time on a real farm. We picked and ate apples actually growing on trees. We ate handfuls of chokecherries too. We saw squirrels for the first time, and even white-tailed deer, which came out to graze with our grandfather's cows. Cliff swallows built nests of dried mud under the eaves of the old barn beside the house. We tried to learn to swim in the "crick" which was part of the Saint John River, and we helped to harvest hay on the "interval" which separated the crick from the rest of the river. Along the main channel, beyond the interval, we used to see the motor vessel *Purdy* churning her way up and down river, carrying passengers between Saint John and Fredericton.

The farm had its own ferry, a flat scow with rails, and a cable running over its deck, operated by a hand winch. It could carry cattle, horses, hay and farm machinery between the mainland and the interval. The ferry also had an attached fish trap from which we sometimes collected fresh water fish—usually, I think, whitefish.

The farm also had a cooperage, where our grandfather and his elder son Ralph made apple barrels. Vina and her sister Madge went swimming with us, but the one who spent the most time with us was our young uncle, Carl Maidment, then a boy of twelve, who seemed to us half a man, and who knew just about everything from how to shoe a horse to how to repair an engine, and who could almost knock a squirrel out of a tree with a green apple.

Madge was the most vivid member of the family, a flapper who went to dances with endless strings of boyfriends, gave herself "permanent waves" with curling irons heated in the stove, and had a collection of pop records that she played on a wind-up record player in the front room. The words of "Moonlight on the River Colorado" are still present among the useless lumber at the back of my mind. Madge worked at a general store in Gagetown, helping the family to struggle through the Great Depression. But we had no concept, at the time, that any struggle was taking place. Stanley Maidment had little luck with his buying and selling of farms and houses and his endless wandering. Before the Depression was over he was forced to sell the farm—his third—and head back to Newfoundland, where my father helped him get a menial job in a brewery owned by the Hickman family.

At the end of summer Andrew took his holidays and arrived at the farm in a new Model A Ford that he had shipped from St. John's to Halifax, then driven on to Gagetown. He and Vina and Madge then took off on a great adventure to Boston, and returned a week later with tales of Revere Beach and the wonders of amusement parks and big city shops. On that trip Madge and Vina contracted a fascination with things American that they never got over. "How the Americans say it" and "how the Americans do it" became part of their daily speech. Madge eventually married an American chiropractor, and spent the rest of her life in the land of her dreams.

The one really lovable member of that family was my grandmother, Minnie Noble. Just as I can think of nothing good to say about her husband Stanley, I can think of nothing ill to say about Minnie. She was warm, kindly, intelligent, and drawn toward the gentler and finer things of life. Wherever she went she grew flowers. She used to paint and draw. As a young woman around the end of the nineteenth century she took up photography and had her own darkroom. Vina always believed that whatever small talent I had as a writer or artist I had inherited from her mother. Captain John would have had a different opinion. Perhaps I inherited something from both grandparents, along with a bit of sheer worldly practicality from the Burkes. Grandmother Maidment was a wonderful woman with children—kind, considerate, always trying to do something for us. I have wondered recently how she must have suffered from following her husband to the eleven different sites in North America where he tried to put down roots, ending, at last, in Minnesota.

When we were small children cars were still a great status symbol. Horses were the commonest transportation in St. John's. The electric street railway was limited to paralleling the waterfront. Trucks were common. "Victoria" carriages, with high back seats and canvas tops, were used as taxis, mainly between the railway station and the hotels. In summer there were buggies, in winter side sleighs with strings of jingling bells attached to the harness.

There were big, square horse-drawn bread wagons and light delivery wagons for meats and vegetables. Coal—the universal fuel—travelled in two-wheeled carts in summer and box-shaped sleds in winter. We watched the heavy, flat-bedded transports called slovens hauling supplies past our gate to The Ropewalk, their teams of huge Belgians and Percherons sweating under the lashes of the drovers.

All the horses were whipped, of course, some excessively, depending on the driver or the owner, or the owner's young sons, some of whom thought whipping horses was great sport, but the big draught horses were treated with systematic cruelty, their tails docked or tightly braided to get them out of the way of the drovers' whips, which were often knotted or weighted with lead shot to make them strike harder. Captain John might express disgust with a man who ill-treated a horse, but there was no general objection to the endless punishment of the horses that went on daily on the streets. I have often wondered whether the abuse of horses in this way did not contribute largely to the callousness that seemed to pervade society as a whole in that era when boys and teenagers were birched at the prison almost every day for minor offenses, and schoolchildren were frequently beaten with leather straps in front of their classes.

At a few road junctions around the city and in Bowring Park there were very ornate cast iron horse cisterns, with lions' heads spitting water into shell-shaped bowls holding ten gallons or more. Near street level there were little drinking bowls for dogs. A few business places had iron hitching posts set up in front. As horses became fewer in St. John's, the house sparrows starved, declining from the tens of thousands that inhabited the city in the early thirties to the few hundred that live there today, no longer as scavengers, but as mendicants at feeding stations.

By the end of the thirties the delivery horse was becoming rare, and by the late forties was regarded as a relic, the two or three still in use photographed and written up in the papers as curiosities. Finally only the riding horse and the racing horse, toys of the wealthy, remained in the city, though outport people continued—and still continue today—to use the small, shaggy native ponies for such jobs as gardening and hauling firewood.

In my experience the outport horse has a pretty easy time of it, usually treated more like a pet than a slave, often living to an astonishing age. One that sometimes hauled firewood for me at Beachy Cove was well over thirty, still fairly sound, and was able and willing to haul spruce and fir logs so long as the loads were light and the pace slow. That horse never needed to be whipped or threatened or spoken to in a harsh voice. If a slope was icy or a bridge looked unsound, I'd walk ahead of him, leading him by the head to give him confidence. Once on an icy slope I lost my footing and actually fell down in front of the horse. He then stood there in a state of absolute terror, trembling all over, like someone who'd seen God fall from heaven.

The small herd of cows we kept on Campbell Avenue numbered never less than four or more than six. My brother and I first milked cows on our grandfather's farm in New Brunswick. When we returned, we were assigned a cow each to milk morning and evening. Lillian milked one, and Andrew one or two, depending on how many were on hand. When our Cousin Bob came visiting from the outports, he milked a cow as well.

Each of us had a special relationship with "his own" cow. Mine was named Nell, an Ayreshire with a docile, even friendly disposition, and the best milker we ever owned. At the peak of her lactation she'd give nine imperial gallons of milk daily. We pastured our cows on a large rented field owned by the Ebsary family. Later a subsidized housing project, known as the Ebsary Estate, was built there, peopled by widows and orphans from condemned houses in the downtown core.

The chores connected with the dairy were divided among family members. Aunt Anne took the cows back and forth to pasture. Lillian ran the cream separator. Grandmother Leah scalded milk, skimmed it for Devonshire cream, and occasionally made the surplus into butter. Lillian and Vina bottled the milk and sold it to neighbours at the back door. Andrew made some deliveries by car, sometimes helped by the kids. When there was more milk than we could retail, he took it to a large dairy connected with a margarine factory about half a mile from our house. Andrew once estimated that the profits from the cows added about $500 a year to the family income, in addition to the milk and cream and butter that we ate ourselves.

In midsummer we made hay on a rented field across the road from our house. Mowed down with a scythe, it was raked, turned, and cured in the sun until it could be loaded on carts and hauled to the hayloft in the barn. My earliest memory of the hayfield is of its marvellous scent, and of the dried flowers sprinkled through the hay. Some of them were deep indigo—half a lifetime later I would learn they were purple vetch—a colour that reminded me of the tiny blue medicine bottles sold in the stores, with essence of ginger and castor oil and sweet spirits of nitre.

Bits of hay got inside your shirt and shorts, and you had to take everything off and pick it out. Later we jumped into the hay piles in the loft, though this was said to be dangerous because someone might have left a hayfork hidden there, and if you jabbed it into yourself you'd get blood poisoning or lockjaw and die in the most frightful agony. Captain John knew of someone in Carbonear who'd got lockjaw some time back in the last century, and the poor mortal died with his head bent right back touching his heels.

Now and then there were rats in the hayloft. They'd come out at night to gnaw holes in the wooden bins and eat the linseed meal and molaseen kept for the cows. But Andrew thought of a plan to fix *them*. He half-filled a barrel with water, covered it with stiff white paper, and slit the paper crosswise with a razor blade. Then he planted it below the hayloft at the foot of the ladder. Any rat that jumped on it would fall through. The paper would then snap back into place, ready for the next victim. Sure enough, next morning he collected three or four drowned or half-drowned rats, but after that they learned to avoid the barrel.

Later we owned a small rat terrier named Cato. This animal formed a successful hunting partnership with Grandmother Leah's tabby cat. The dog would ferret the rat out of its hiding place; then, as it dashed for new cover, the cat would pounce and finish it off. The rats took to nesting in the eaves, where the dog could not reach them, but Andrew discovered that you could flush them out by throwing cold water into the eaves. They'd leap out in terror and land on the floor where either the cat or dog would get them. More than forty rats met their ends in this way on one memorable weekend. For months afterwards no one could find a rat anywhere on the property.

Chapter 5

When I started school in 1931 the Great Depression had not yet reached its depths in Newfoundland. It came a year or two late to the Oldest Colony because the collapse depended on the failure of markets for fish, paper and minerals—failures that didn't occur right on the heels of the Wall Street Crash. But by the early months of 1932, the worst of the Great Hunger was beginning to be felt.

In the 1930s, once the Great Depression had settled over the land, all the roads leading into St. John's from the countryside had men and dogs hauling sled-loads of firewood in winter. The sled used was usually the Newfoundland catamaran, and usually there was just the one big dog pulling, and the man to help push when they were going uphill. The same kind of sled was hauled by small horses in the outports, but of course almost nobody in the city owned a horse.

City people "on the dole" could get an order for a quarter of a ton of soft coal, which might be enough to keep a cooking fire going in the kitchen, but provided little enough for heat. There was still some crown land where people could cut firewood. Parish priests would often allow woodcutting on church lands, and many private owners of forest land would also allow it. So there was always a place to cut spruce and fir, provided you could get it home.

This was also a time of public vegetable lots. Again, outport people were better off because most of them had small garden plots where they could grow a few vegetables. The government secured permission from the owners of vacant land inside the city, and measured off sections where people could grow potatoes, turnips and cabbages—the three staples of Newfoundland gardens. Those in the suburbs often kept a few hens, feeding them table scraps, and grain if they could afford it.

A lot of ragged and cast-off clothing was in evidence in those years, but even the veriest ragamuffin in the city had some kind of a pair of boots. Thousands of outport children went barefoot. City children did not—at least, not downtown. It would have been seen as the very depth of indigence for any boy to be walking on the road without boots, and somebody would be sure to find him a cast-off pair. As long as they were big enough, what matter if they didn't fit? There was little begging on the streets, but a lot from door to door, where endless slices of bread were handed out by housewives. People "on the dole" were close to starvation. A family of five could qualify for a food order worth, as a rule, $2.10 a week, but this couldn't possibly provide even minimum subsistence.

Newfoundland was an independent country, deeply in debt, with pitiably small revenues. The government, of course, was blamed. And when it was revealed that the Prime Minister, Sir Richard Squires, had been dabbling in graft (probably to finance the Liberal Party, though he was said to be "fattening his own pocket"), a mob of some ten thousand unemployed men marched on the Colonial Building, where the legislature was in session, smashed the windows, started a bonfire with some of the furniture, including a piano, pulled down the Union Jack and ran up some kind of green flag in its place. They tried to lynch the Prime Minister, and probably would have thrown him into the harbour if they could have got their hands on him, but he was hustled away by a small group of supporters, the mob howling at his heels, across Military Road to Colonial Street, where a priest, Father Joseph Pippy, stood in a doorway, arms outspread, keeping the mob back while Squires was pushed inside, then out the back door, over a fence and into another back door, and out of the front of that house to Bannerman Street, where a car picked him up and drove him away.

The mob then rioted along Duckworth and Water Streets, looted a government liquor store, and ended the night drunk in the gutters.

The governor had the riot act read, to no effect, and cabled Great Britain for assistance. The British diverted their nearest warship, a cruiser, to St. John's, but it would take several days to arrive. Meanwhile the government "swore in" a squad of special police (mostly war veterans) who began controlling the city. The schools remained open, and, oddly enough, though I was only eight years old, I was allowed to roam about the streets and observe all the excitement. The next day there were still crowds of unemployed men milling about downtown, but nothing that could be called a mob.

To cap the drama the warship arrived in the harbour, bristling with heavy guns. If necessary, she could have put a thousand well-armed men on the streets, but everything remained quiet, the threat of revolution faded, and the hunger and the hopelessness returned.

Squires resigned, and the Tories took the government in a landslide with only two outport seats going to the Liberals. The new government soon applied to Britain for the suspension of Dominion status. The formalities took well over a year, but early in 1934 Government by Commission, with three Newfoundlanders, three experienced British civil servants, and the British Governor, was sworn into office, and ran the country for fifteen years, providing what was probably the best government the country had ever enjoyed. Poverty remained, but small economic schemes such as land settlement and logging for export took care of some of the unemployed, and the Great Depression ended in Newfoundland well before the outbreak of the Second World War.

Starting school in our society is a major rite of passage, like circumcision among the Arabs or dream-fasting among the Amerindians. The horror was postponed for me until I was nearly seven years old because Vina and Andrew decided it would be less of a nuisance if they started their two sons in school the same year instead of a year apart.

So when Charlie was five years and four months and I was six years and ten months we started school together in the same classroom—for one day. On discovering that I could already read a little the teacher moved me to what would now be called grade one.

Long before I went to school Great-aunt Anne had been teaching me to write by letting me hold a pencil while she "guided my hand" as she expressed it, forming the letters for me, a method used in her own infancy for passing literacy from parent to child in the numerous places where schools did not exist, but where, nonetheless, every self-respecting person learned to read and write. So when I started school I could already write simple sentences in cursive script if someone told me how to spell every other word.

It wasn't the business of learning that shocked me, or the sudden transfer to the alien authority of the teacher. The teachers in those first two grades at Holloway School were marvellously understanding and kind. Mine was a Miss Dingle who, in her old age, quite justly received a national honour for her life work with children. She managed her class with a calm assured authority that made punishment of any kind absolutely unnecessary. The shock at first was not the teachers, but the children.

Our parents had decided to send us to Holloway School, the "upper-class" school of the United Church Board of Education where the fees charged to parents were much higher than those at the lower-class schools on Bond Street and Parade Street and elsewhere in the city. We must have had this impressed on us, because we carried through childhood a fixed impression that our school housed a distinctly higher class of people than the grubby kids who went to those inferior schools.

How different the classes and the masses might have been I'm not now sure. We picked up head lice at Holloway School, and Vina bought fine-toothed combs and tar soap to deal with them. We also caught most of the childhood diseases of the time: measles, mumps, whooping cough, German measles and chicken pox. Immunization against smallpox and diphtheria were by then bringing them under control, and typhoid fever had been nearly eliminated by clean water and milk and public sanitation. But the "childhood diseases" were still pandemic.

At Holloway you did get a little extra for the higher school fees. The teachers were a little better paid and better educated. There was a visiting art teacher who taught elementary drawing and colouring. There was a music teacher who taught you singing and also piano if you paid an extra fee. There was a gym teacher. When you reached grade five you got a weekly class of cooking or "manual training" ("shop" in current slang) depending on your sex. The carpentry was taught in a special room in the basement of the upper school, Prince of Wales College, nearly a mile from the elementary school, so the grade five boys paraded back and forth once a week. The cooking class was taught at Holloway School by a visiting teacher.

We greatly enjoyed the manual training class, even if we didn't learn much from it. In addition to common hand tools there were a drill press, a power saw, and a wood-turning lathe. Perhaps some of the boys more clever with their hands than I got to use those sophisticated appliances—I'm not sure. I was never very good at manual training.

There were other extras, too, including something called "elocution" for kids whose parents thought they needed it. I still don't know whether you went to elocution because you stuttered, or because you pronounced your words like a St. John's corner boy. In any case, it was supposed to teach you to speak correctly, to use the "King's English," as the teachers said.

For children who had been raised in a Christian family where the Sermon on the Mount was the rule of life, even if it was often ignored, the real shock of starting school was the sudden plunge into the barbarian society of the playroom and the schoolyard, among children who had been taught from birth, by precept and example, that life was a jungle, everyone red in tooth and claw and the devil taking the hindmost. There was no supervision in playroom or playground. The savages were left, outside the classroom, entirely to their own devices.

By grade two the jungle came into the classroom, where nothing really mattered except placing first, second, third or thirtieth, and everyone's standing was public knowledge. Worse still, achievement in the classroom was of little importance compared with your standing in such gladiator sports as football and hockey. Some boys were instant successes in these games. I was an adult before I realized that their fathers had been training them for the football field and the hockey rink from the day they took their first steps.

So far as teachers were concerned, the shock also came in grade two, in a class where the teacher rapped the boys' fingers with a ruler for minor mistakes, and lined them up by the blackboard to get the strap when they made more than three errors in their daily spelling tests.

That was the level at which boys and girls were segregated into classes at opposite ends of the school, an arrangement that would continue until grade eleven, when some classes once more would be co-educational. Perhaps the frequency of corporal punishment was one of the reasons for this; girls may have been thought too refined and delicate to watch boys, day after day, being punished with the ruler and the strap.

As a matter of fact, the strapping was rarely severe. I got strapped only once in that school, and to my great surprise discovered that it wasn't unbearably painful; like many other boys, I could take it without shedding a tear. The actual pain was not so horrendous as the constant threat of it. And there was always the further threat of being sent to the principal, the dreadful Miss Fanny Badcock, for a *real* whipping, from which you'd come back with your eyes red and your hands swollen. For the final, ultimate crime, such as playing hookey, even Fanny Badcock might be incapable of inflicting sufficient agony. In that case, the burly male principal from the senior school would come for a visit, bringing his strap with him, and the offender would be hauled off to the office to be reduced to the appropriate state of whimpering contrition.

Parents almost universally approved of terror in the classroom. Humane teachers worked in an environment where terrorism was practised as a matter of course next door. In grade four we had a teacher who never whipped anybody and certainly never sent anyone to Miss Badcock; who came back voluntarily on Saturday mornings to help us carry out experiments with sprouting seeds and developing tadpoles. She had a degree in science, and I suppose had majored in biology, but what she taught us on Saturdays, what we came voluntarily to do in a school that was otherwise a prison, was not regarded as education, but as a variety of extra-curricular fun, like cub scouts and brownies.

There were no school buses. Most kids walked. Others, from well-heeled families, rode bicycles, Hercules and Raleighs, heavy ungeared machines from England. My brother and I usually arrived by car and departed on foot; I believe we were the only kids whose mother sometimes picked them up with a horse and buggy, which was fun, and conferred its own odd kind of status.

Kids not only walked back and forth to school, often half an hour or more each way, but most men walked to work. Almost everyone walked to church. We accepted the cosmology of Copernicus, but otherwise held much the same beliefs as Martin Luther. We sang the songs our grandparents had sung in their youth.

The few modern things we owned—a car, a radio, a primitive washing machine—hadn't really changed our lives much. Looking back at the twenties and thirties the thing that strikes me most forcefully is how little change there had been. It was still the Dream Time, the world before the present world began, the world as it had been through infinite layers of the past. My great uncle caught and cured fish for a living, using gear that had been improved a little in the previous century, but not in any radical way. Basically, he worked with the tools his ancestors had brought to Carbonear three centuries before.

The odd miracle came fluttering by, but had not yet reached down into our lives. We saw Lindbergh fly over St. John's, and I dreamed of flying off Quidi Vidi Lake like Captain Douglas Fraser and Arthur

Sullivan, but the thought that I would one day fly non-stop to Vancouver, Moscow, Trinidad or Baffin Island never once entered my mind.

Because most kids got to school on their own, there was great fuss about what the teachers called "punctuality." If you were late, you ran full tilt to try to beat the second bell, for if you came slinking into class after a lesson was already in progress you might get the strap.

Though the school was managed by a board appointed by the United Church of Canada, successor to the Methodists, that didn't mean that there was any religious instruction in the curriculum. There was an assembly in the auditorium each morning. We sang a hymn. The principal read something or other—a chapter from the Bible, I suppose. Then there might be a short bit of classical music on a big record player, after which we would recite the Lord's prayer and sing another hymn. The whole thing took perhaps twenty minutes. That was our education in religion, ethics and aesthetics, all rolled into one. We were then dismissed to our classrooms to spend the rest of the day as barbarians. The Roman Catholic schools actually made an effort to teach the particular superstitions and falsehoods to which Catholics are supposed to adhere; our school made no such effort.

In my second or third year I discovered a small trace of competitive ability in athletics. Though I could never kick a ball straight or skate well, and hence could never rank anywhere in the two sports that *really* mattered, it turned out that I could run, and even win prizes for it. This was some small compensation in a social order where I was otherwise near the bottom of the heap. Later, in high school, I also discovered a talent for basketball. But these things didn't really count. The things that established the pecking order were football (called "soccer" in North America, where "football" is played with the hands rather than the feet) and hockey. I happened also, by some fluke, to be the best cricket player in the school, and made a "century" with the coach bowling against me, truly astonished that he was unable to bowl me out. In an English school, I suppose, I might have become an athletic hero. In St. John's it counted for absolutely nothing; it was just a curiosity, like being able to wiggle your ears or shoot marbles with your toes.

Classroom standing was determined by adding up the results of weekly tests, mainly in spelling and arithmetic. In the early grades I was about seventeenth out of thirty-two to thirty-five boys. Then, in grade five, I crept up to thirteenth the second term, and ninth the final term, making it—barely—into the "top ten" who were considered to have some prospects. Because I behaved myself and did my work, I made it all the way through the grade five class run by the dreadful Miss Fanny Badcock without ever getting her cane across the legs or her strap across the hands. The one time she was planning to give me a whipping, for ducking out of a detention class where I was being kept unjustly, she slipped on the ice and broke her arm, and went off to hospital. The gods who ruled the pagan world of the school must have been on my side that winter.

Fanny Badcock was an appallingly bad teacher, far too handy with the cane and the strap, and the subject of a schoolboy rhyme:

> Old Fanny Badcock,
> She goes to church on Sunday
> And prays the Lord to give her strength
> To whip the boys on Monday.

Even worse than her fondness for whipping was her habit of heaping abuse on those who could not do their sums correctly or write their assignments. She used to rant at those who did badly, call them "dullards" and "nincompoops," tell them their "mentalities" were sub-normal, and predict that they'd wind up as ditch-diggers. Sometimes she'd add that it was all the fault of their families. Since I was never subjected to this, I can only guess what it may have done to boys who lacked my family background with its assured self-confidence. It must surely have helped to destroy their self-image, if they ever had any. It now seems almost incredible that such a woman, so equipped by temperament to do the maximum amount of damage to any child placed under her, should have been chosen by a supposedly responsible board to be the head of a school of some 350 children between the ages of five and eleven. And yet it wasn't unusual; even as late as the 1950s and '60s some of the school principals at St. John's were obvious sadists who got sexual thrills from whipping children.

So what did we learn? Well, we learned the three Rs, most of us, those who would have learned them anyway. And we learned to cheat, to lie, to be dishonest with our parents as well as our teachers, for they were in conspiracy against us. We learned that the adult world was our enemy. We learned that all this was "natural," "human nature," that you spent twenty minutes a day pretending to believe in a set of principles that you completely repudiated the rest of the time. We were being taught to accept our place—whatever it might be—in nineteenth century capitalist society. We were being taught to kill and be killed in the Second World War. That was the reality behind the hypocrisy.

In grade six I made the astonishing discovery that I was "the smartest kid in the class." Instead of getting marks for weekly tests, we now for the first time wrote term-end examinations. Then my phenomenal memory for anything I had read even once, combined with my facility in reading and writing, gave me a previously unsuspected advantage. When the exams were all marked and totalled, the teacher asked me to stand up and tell her where I'd placed the year before.

"Ninth last term, Miss, fourteenth for the year."

"Well, this term you've placed first," she said.

I actually felt dizzy with surprise, and it must have been a great shock to the two or three boys who had always considered that they were the only ones in the competition. I didn't continue to place first all the time, but I placed first for the year, and from then on I was among the top three. Most important: I did it without effort. While the others swatted over their books at home I read John Buchan's novels.

A couple of grades later, when we graduated from arithmetic to geometry and algebra, I discovered an equally surprising talent for theoretical mathematics and logic. So I went through the upper school winning prizes and scholarships without ever making the slightest effort to do so, and hated every minute of it. Or almost every minute. Not quite. The science class could be a joy. Basketball was great fun. And by then there were warm, even romantic, friendships to lighten the surrounding gloom.

During the winter of my first year at school I came down with the one life-threatening illness of my childhood. Many children then died in infancy, and quite a few others died before reaching their teens. Meningitis was one killer. Pneumonia was another. Mastoid infections were a third. Tuberculosis killed boys and girls in their teens (one of my classmates died this way) but most TB victims were among the poor, or from homes that practised bad nutrition. The principal threat in our family seemed to come from influenza and its complications. With me it was a prolonged and stubborn ear infection, following a cold and a cough.

After such home remedies as dropping hot olive oil into the ear had failed, the doctor was called in. The infection involved some pain, a rupture of the left eardrum, and draining that went on for a long time. I spent most of that time in bed. Looking back, it seems like about six weeks, but I suppose, allowing for memory distortion, it may have been two weeks.

Most such illnesses were treated at home by visiting doctors. Only when you were likely to die were you moved to hospital. Two doctors attended me, the family M.D., Dr. Grieve, and an "eye, ear, nose and throat specialist," Dr. Smith. Of course there were no antibiotics, so there was no way of treating such infections through the bloodstream. Topical treatments, heat and "building up your resistance" were the approach, with surgery as a last resort. If an inner ear infection spread to the mastoid bone, the only effective treatment was surgery, and the survival rate from the operation was approximately fifty percent.

I was treated with some kind of bitter medicine, taken by mouth, and by dropping alcohol into the ear itself, afterwards allowing it to drain. At one point the doctor told Vina to get me ready for the hospital, which presumably would mean the mastoid operation and the fifty-fifty chance of dying, but by the next day I seemed to be better; my fever was down a point or two. Gradually, the draining from the ear ceased. And for a wonder, my hearing was not affected.

Vina, in any case, was always playing doctor, dosing us with this and that, much of it harmless, some of it harmful. Her strong anal fixation didn't end with toilet training, by any means, or with poking a bakelite probe up a toddler's anus to check for constipation; she went on to see that everybody had regular bowel movements, or if not regular, at least generous. She purged us first with a children's laxative called Castoria, and later with the much stronger poison called senna tea. If we caught a cold, her first reaction was to give us the shits on top of it. She had a theory that this would carry the cold down though your digestive tract, and out through your arse. Senna tea, especially, was an article of faith, and many a time we were forced to drink the abominable stuff, followed, a few hours later, by horrible digestive cramps and the misery of diarrhoea.

This treatment had no effect on the cold, which progressed from nose to throat to chest with a cough that seemed to go on forever. We were sick with colds, every year, from late autumn to late spring. There were, even then, medicines useful in the treatment of chest colds, medicines such as expectorants, and sometimes we received small, ineffective doses of Dr. Chase's Cough Medicine. We also had our chests rubbed with goose grease. I'm not sure whether this had any effect or not. Later we were treated with mustard plasters, and these, by burning your skin over an area of congestion, may really have done some good—the same kind of effect you get from a heating pad. Vina, however, had a theory that what you needed was not just something to increase the blood supply to an affected region, but overall stimulation of the circulation, so she applied mustard plasters not only to our chests, but also to the soles of our feet.

We were fed various tonics. Every winter we had cod liver oil. Nothing wrong with that. You get a little vitamin D from cod liver oil at a season when you get little of it from the sunlight, and vitamin A, also in cod liver, is useful in treating or preventing chest cold, but a teaspoonful once a day, the way we got it, has little effect.

When we objected to the vile flavour of cod liver oil we were allowed to have Scott's Emulsion instead. It was supposed to have the same vitamins in relatively palatable form.

Parish's Chemical Food was another nostrum that we received regularly. It was pleasant, and we enjoyed taking it. It probably contained iron, in one form or another, and was strong on phosphates. We probably weren't phosphorous-deficient, but there was a popular belief in the magic properties of this element at the time.

The one nutrient in which we were certainly drastically deficient was vitamin C. We probably went for weeks at a time with no more of it than we might get from our mashed potatoes, or perhaps an occasional orange. Nothing was known, then, about vitamin C except that a mere trace of it prevented scurvy, and this mere trace was officially said to be enough. When I think of the six-month bouts of misery that we endured every year, the inevitable bronchitis, inner ear infections that threatened our hearing and even our lives, and when I compare this with the immunity enjoyed by my own children, who are rarely sick longer than one day, I'm appalled by the nutritional ignorance that plagued my childhood.

Every spring we received doses of sulphur mixed with molasses. This was "to clean your blood" and get you ready for the active months ahead. Needless to say, its only real effect was to make you fart like a chemical factory.

A few traditional remedies were useful. Honey was used for a sore mouth. It is, in fact, a mild and edible disinfectant. Black currant jam, often mixed into a warm drink, was used for a sore throat and a cold. It contains fairly large amounts of vitamin C. A pity it wasn't used in much larger quantities. Daily rations of black currant jam might well have made a substantial difference to our lives. Unfortunately, instead of being used as a regular food, it was kept as an emergency nostrum. We grew black currants in our yard and, instead of a mere couple of quarts a year, could easily have grown them by the bushel.

The traditional knowledge, such as it was, came from our grandparents. I don't think Vina had much faith in it. She preferred her own theories of increasing the circulation and opening the bowels, and never seemed to lose faith in her system even though it never worked, or at least never worked very well. As soon as we were old enough to rebel against her authority we refused to drink any more senna tea, or to take any other of her range of "opening medicines." Thus we escaped lifelong constipation and lifelong addiction to laxatives. I have not taken a laxative since the age of eleven, and have no intention of taking one in the future. I regard them as a pure curse created by quacks.

Besides home-grown quackery, we were subject to some extent to the quackery of the medical profession. But we escaped the quackery of tonsillectomies at a time when doctors were fattening their pockets by performing this disgraceful piece of useless and dangerous surgery on just about anyone who would submit to it. A travelling nurse looked down everyone's throat at school and sent home a note recommending that the tonsils be cut out. If they looked large, or if the throat looked a bit inflamed, they were supposed to be a "centre of infection." I don't know whether the nurses got kickbacks from the surgeons or not, but it wouldn't surprise me in the least. Luckily, our parents believed that all human organs performed a useful function. They believed that tonsils were intended to trap infection and prevent it from spreading (which is very close indeed to the truth) and so refused to have us subjected to this harmful surgery that enriched thousands of doctors and damaged millions of children and adults, and even killed a few of them, in the first half of the twentieth century.

Not all of Vina's theories were nonsense. She had faith in natural foods and whole grains half a century or more before the first "natural food store" began stocking yogurt and wheat germ. She made her own bread—the only bread eaten in our house. It contained whole wheat flour, molasses, potatoes and milk. She even went in for such natural food supplements as kelp when you couldn't buy them anywhere except by mail order. Her faith in natural foods, at a time when it was scorned as "fadism," was probably one of the reasons she lived into her mid-eighties, and her husband into his early nineties. Andrew outlived both his parents and his grandparents, despite the stresses of modern life, the pollutants of the city environment, and the fact that he never took any exercise in the latter half of his life, or anyway nothing more than a half-mile stroll on a city sidewalk. He outlived his mother by two years, and his father by eleven. He had never been overweight, and always looked healthy. Vina's "food fadism" may well have extended his life by ten years.

Throughout early childhood we were constantly given candy as treats. By the age of four my milk teeth were in bad enough shape that my parents decided some of them should be extracted to prevent the infection of permanent teeth forming underneath. So I was taken to a dentist. Because of an all-pervasive fear of dentistry, I was expected to face the ordeal in fear and trembling. To help steel me for it, I was given a new toy on the way to the surgery—a brightly striped noise maker on a stick that clicked loudly when you swung it around.

I have no idea how many teeth were extracted, because I was knocked out with chloroform, and woke up vomiting what looked like buckets of blood into a basin. The experience, in fact, wasn't terrifying, and in spite of the dentist-terror that prevailed in our family, visits to dentists have never bothered me at all.

The one irrational fear that was successfully transmitted to me was a fear of insects. Grandmother Leah was particularly adept at this. She called the harmless tiger beetles that ran about in our barn "hornets," and was free with stories about the horrible black and blue swellings suffered by people who had been "bitten" by them. When, as an adult, I began to take an interest in the natural world, I had to *train* myself to overcome the phobia, to recognize that nearly all insects are harmless to humans, and quite safe to handle. Gradually I gained an admiration and affection for their intricate beauty that would have been regarded as foolhardy and unnatural in my childhood.

Among the "extras" in my education was music. At one time or another I played both the piano and the violin very badly. Our family had a strong belief that it was "musical." They sang in choirs, played in bands. Some could play the piano. Andrew played the violin after a fashion. Sam played the cornet and the organ, much better. Many of them could sing a line of music off the page, or play four-part music from a sheet. They enjoyed sing-alongs. So when they discovered that by the age of ten I could play any tune I knew on the piano, and improvise a four-part harmony with it, they assumed that all the enormous family talent was coming to fruit. They taught me the notes, taught me to spell out a tune from written music, and by the age of twelve I was condemned to take lessons on the piano, so escaping the regular classroom once a week to visit the music teacher and practise scales.

That, I'm sure, was the trouble. The teachers were good pianists themselves, could play beautifully. But they treated me like an idiot child. Instead of discussing harmonic progressions, as they might have, or explaining the relationships between major and minor keys—which I later had to discover for myself—they made me do meaningless "exercises" of triplets and other musical baby-talk, and they set lessons to be practised at home. I never did the lessons.

One of my teachers discovered that I had an excellent sense of pitch, and could name any note he struck on the piano without looking. This, according to the ideas of the time, set me in a special class. He told my father that I had the makings of a professional musician if I'd only work at it. But I refused. I would not sit at the piano and do the dum-dum-dums that were expected of me. In the end they gave me up as a failure, thank God. Not that I would ever have become a professional musician, even if the music lessons had succeeded. That was my father's ambition for me, not mine.

It is perfectly true that I was lazy. I shirked all my lessons, not just the finger exercises on the piano. Music should be fun. Reading should be fun. Science and math should be fun. I refused to memorize formulae in math or in physics. Even the formula for quadratic equations was one I refused to memorize. If I needed it in an exam, I worked it out from scratch, as quickly as I could. I still don't know the formula for a falling body, but I can calculate its velocity at any point in its trajectory just the same.

The life of the run-of-the-mill performing artist appals me. Swatting at any piece of work, over and over again, eight and ten hours a day, world without end, is not a good way to live. As well to work on the rock pile. Glenn Gould was an exception. But then, he was a genius who never had to swat. If a musician can't be a Glenn Gould he should do something else for a living, and play music for the joy of it, as Gould did. I had no compunction, as an adult, in letting Gould hear me play. We both knew that I was having fun, not aiming for expertise. We both knew that my playing could never reach concert level, and that I had found something else that I could do far better. The old saw about genius being nine-tenths perspiration is sheer nonsense. The best things are effortless, and don't just *appear* to be. Gould's playing, and my writing, were very nearly effortless. And I know better than any critic which of my books are the best—the ones that gave me no trouble, the ones that were fun to write.

Occasionally I'm interviewed, and asked about my work habits. It's difficult to answer truthfully because I don't have any work habits, except to avoid work as much as possible. How much time do I spend writing? I don't know. I do it in fits and starts, sometimes twelve or fourteen hours a day, sometimes not at all for weeks or even months at a stretch, but I don't think, averaged over the past thirty years and twenty-five books, that I've spent two days a week working.

Music, for me, was going to be work, and I'm damn glad I avoided it, even at the cost of being a dire disappointment to my poor father.

Chapter 6

When I was eight years old the extended family split up, and the typical North American group—mother, father and two kids—moved off to the shell of a new bungalow on Oxen Pond Road ("in the woods" as Great-aunt Anne scornfully called it). There we worked day and night to finish the house and make it habitable. After my first night in the bungalow I awoke beside an open window with a wonderful feeling of refreshment and well-being. It must have been early summer, possibly mid-June. I had rarely felt such euphoria.

The move from Campbell Avenue to Oxen Pond Road was a move to a wholly new world of myth. Here we were plunged into raw nature, almost wilderness, surrounded by woods and streams and lakes and ponds, a hill that had just the touch of the character of a mountain, and a small river that rose somewhere in the back of beyond and ran off through distant lakes and steadies and over roaring waterfalls to the far-away sea. Here we became cowboys and pirates and naked Indians; here we learned to run barefoot through the woods and fields, to climb trees, to build bow-houses, to swim in shallow river pools, and eventually to swim across full-sized lakes.

Vina, of course, had insisted on the move to "the country"—actually barely a mile from Campbell Avenue, but separated from it by solid blocks of woodland. The quarter acre that they bought on Oxen Pond Road was only a few hundred yards from the farm that Vina remembered from her girlhood, a farm where she could still point out the grave of her pet rabbit. All her life she continued to have a yearning for "the country," pulling Andrew off toward the fringes, while he kept pulling back toward the city.

There must have been a lot of tension between Vina and the Horwoods. She must have disliked Captain John intensely, though she never said a lot about it. She cordially detested Great-aunt Anne. Because Aunt Anne had a weak chest, and suffered from frequent bouts of flu, Vina told us that she suspected the woman had a chronic low-grade case of tuberculosis, and should be avoided. It was the sort of groundless fantasy about health that Vina indulged in all her life. And, of course, in the 1930s tuberculosis was still a major killer, especially of young people. She also suspected some of our neighbours of syphilis, and told us so—again with no grounds except that they were thin and poor and seemed sickly.

The move to Oxen Pond Road was a move to primitive living conditions. We had a shallow well with a hand pump, dug right beside the house. Soon there was a side veranda built over it, so that you had a good supply of water almost but not quite indoors. Instead of a backhouse, a privy occupied a corner of the two-car garage, which was used as a storehouse for just about everything that would normally be kept in a basement. I remember the privy as a noisome hole, always stinking (completely unnecessary, since a handful of lime or a shovelful of earth tossed into a privy after each use will keep it stench-free).

For baths, we used a washing tub, set on the living room floor, and filled with water warmed on the stove. I don't know when Andrew and Vina took baths—I suppose after we kids were asleep. Neither of our parents ever undressed in our presence, or touched us when we were naked: the taboos concerning the body were total.

When Charlie was eight and I was nearing ten, our sister Ruth was born. Vina went off to St. John's well ahead of the event, to be sure she'd be no more than a few hundred yards from a hospital when labour started. The baby was born August 3, 1933, and Vina enjoyed a nine-day bed rest in hospital before coming home. In the thirties giving birth was regarded as an extreme medical crisis, requiring constant medical intervention and prolonged rest after the event.

Ruth had a far less perverted upbringing than Charlie and I, because her two brothers were old enough to set themselves firmly against Vina's nonsense; we did as much to "raise" her as her parents, and though we were, inevitably, warped by our own early training, we were not nearly as warped as Vina herself. So Ruth became, by comparison, a liberated child, much more like her wild Aunt Madge than her mother. That was the end of Vina's childbearing. Thenceforth she practised rhythm birth control with only one error. Seven years after Ruth's birth she slipped up again, became pregnant and miscarried.

Perhaps the arrival of the baby hastened the business of extending and modernizing the house. Anyway, Andrew built a back wing, which included a new bedroom for Charlie and me, a bathroom and a large back porch. At the same time he put in an electric pumping system, a septic tank, and a hot water boiler. For me the sensual luxury of a truly hot bath was quite a novelty; I'd soak in it for an hour at a time; the bathroom was warmed by a small coal stove which you could stoke to red heat, thus creating the atmosphere of a sauna. For some reason, Vina never realized the sinfulness of such sybaritic luxury, or the fact that such bathing usually included masturbation, which I had suddenly discovered about this time.

In other respects she was still a Spartan. She occasionally whipped us with a piece of cord, never for any offence serious enough for me to recall, and at one point she even persuaded Andrew that he ought to keep a leather strap for discipline, so he brought home a two-foot length of harness leather and housed it on top of the china closet. I think it was only once that he tried to strap me with it, so unconvincingly that I can't remember its hurting at all. After that he forgot it, and it soon disappeared, because I stole it, cut it into short pieces, and threw them into the garbage. Perhaps because his own father had never whipped him, Andrew was quite unsuccessful at child abuse, but equally unsuccessful at loving a child or winning a child's love.

In spite of his gentlemanliness, I wasn't at all fond of him, or of my mother, either. Although she talked about loving us, I never believed her. Indeed, the first sensation of loving or being loved came to me not from inside the family at all, but from among the girls and boys with whom I associated outside the home, from strangers.

I suppose you could say I loved my brother. But we were too close in age—a mere eighteen months—for a true big brother-little brother relationship. We were thick as thieves, did everything together. When I was in grade six I even went to the unheard-of length of asking our teacher to let him come with us on our class excursion to Manuels River (and she agreed). But in general we were more rivals than anything else, and sometimes fought like tigers. Andrew once told me he was afraid we'd kill or seriously injure each other. There was no such rivalry with the friends I made outside the family—nothing but peace and courtesy and mutual good will.

When all the building was complete there were three stoves to heat the bungalow: the kitchen range, the bathroom stove, and a nickel-plated space heater in the sitting room, all burning coal, and though they were not airtight, it was easy to bank the fire with coal dust to make it last all night. The house was built tightly, the seams of inner walls stripped with cloth and paste, the whole covered with a heavy "sheathing paper" before the wallpaper was added. There was a low attic, but no insulation in the roof. Andrew did insulate the walls, in the areas where the plumbing was at risk, using such materials as sawdust and old newspapers, but in general the idea of insulating a house was still a thing of the future. Storm windows were screwed to the outside of the window boxes in winter and removed in spring. Bedrooms all had doors opening into the living room, kitchen or bathroom, and so could take heat from those places. Altogether, the house was reasonably comfortable, even in winter.

Vina made most of our clothes, knitted sweaters, socks and mitts, sewed winter breeches using blue felt-like cloth that was certainly warm, and fairly waterproof. Though we weren't poor compared to our neighbours, she was extremely economical with money, even saving flour sacks, bleaching the print out of them, then sewing them into bed sheets on her foot-powered Singer sewing machine. She may have made pillow slips in this way, too. She made her own dresses and other clothing—all of it. The one thing we bought ready-made was underwear, Stanfield's combinations for winter, shorts and singlets for summer. At one point she even made a blue serge three-piece suit for Andrew, using a ripped-up old suit for a pattern. She made pyjamas for all of us, out of flannelette pound goods.

At some point during those years I began leaving off pyjamas in summer, and sleeping nude. When Vina discovered this, she was shocked.

"You *must* wear pyjamas in bed," she assured me.

"Why?"

She groped for a second, but soon found an answer: "There could be a fire. Then where would you be?"

It seemed to me that in such an emergency going outside wrapped in a sheet would be no great shame, but I didn't argue. I just said OK, and continued to leave my pyjamas under my pillow whenever the weather was warm.

Vina changed slowly, under the influence of her children. By middle age, she began reading novels, including soft porn. She started taking the occasional swallow of wine and even brandy "for her nerves" which were always in need of doctoring. During her first stay on Campbell Avenue she suffered a brief period of bed rest for what she called "a nervous breakdown." Eventually, she kept a regular supply of port on hand. She began spending money on luxuries. Among the things she left behind when she died were several sets of bone china, and a full-length mink coat. But all that would come in the future. In my childhood and early youth she was a prize penny-pincher, and managed to convince me that wasting money was almost as sinful as sex.

Throughout the time of our stay on Oxen Pond Road, the whole valley of Leary's River and the country beside it (cleared and farmed by Irish peasants a couple of generations earlier) remained fairly wild—a mixture of old pasture land and woods. Almost opposite our gate was a small marshy pond where you could skate in winter. A hundred yards down the road was a steep bank for sledding. The fields extended to Thorburn Road, and thence upriver to the waterfalls. Almost nobody else frequented that beautiful upper stretch of the river; it came close to the quality of wilderness, and we loved it in those last years before it was destroyed to make way for warehouses and offices and a shopping mall.

Though the move to the country gave us woods and fields and rivers for our pleasure, life there wasn't all fun. My brother and I drove a lot of nails in that house, helped build and paint the barn, and did most of the dirty work in the poultry house, where our parents kept a flock of a hundred laying hens, as well as hatching several thousand chicks each year.

Layers of wood chips from a planing mill covered the hen house floor, and had to be scraped off with the underlying layer of chicken shit once a month to be piled outside and later incorporated into Vina's vegetable garden. Charlie and I were invariably assigned this filthy task, which we hated. I still despise the stink of a poultry house. Nothing short of actual hunger would induce me to keep a laying hen.

While painting the barn I suffered heat stroke. It was a broiling day in mid-summer, the heat increased by reflection from the white paint that I was laying on. I began to feel as though I might throw up, so I laid down the brush, walked unsteadily to the house, and sat beside an open window. Half an hour later I regained consciousness, still slumped beside the window. When he came home from work that evening Andrew explained that what had happened to me was called sunstroke—I should be careful to wear a cap when working in the sun. So

Vina made white calico skull caps for us. Do they help prevent heat strokes? I don't know.

Charlie and I continued to milk a cow each, morning and evening, driving to our grandparents' house with Andrew, changing into white overalls for milking, changing again for school in the mornings or for the trip home in the evenings. In winter, when the car was put away, we took our coaster sleds, and went sliding down the hills of Stamp's Lane on the way to and from Campbell Avenue. There was no motor traffic and little horse traffic on the road in winter.

After catching me with my paw in the "milk money" to buy a chocolate bar, Andrew decided that both of us should get a share of the profits, so Charlie and I got regular shares, in cash, when the surplus funds from the "milk money" were divided. With these funds my brother and I became Grade School capitalists. Out of our shares we financed a horse, and since our father was manager of a fuel company, selling coal by quarter tons and half tons to houses all over the city, it was easy to get profitable work for the horse. We rode him a little, and drove him a bit, tackled to a buggy, but mainly we hired him out for hauling light loads of coal, too small to be worth the bother of the big cart horses owned by our uncle. Out of the proceeds came the driver's salary and the horse's feed. The rest was divided between my brother and me, and for a while, despite the Great Depression, we were inordinately rich.

I bought my first bicycle, my first cowboy hat, an accordion, a sweater with an incredibly jazzy pattern, and my first pairs of skis, out of the horse's earnings. It gave me a real sense of power to prowl along Water Street, window shopping, knowing that I had the money to buy just about anything that took my fancy.

The bicycle was my first truly thrilling possession. I never did learn to drive a horse properly, mainly, I suppose, because I never learned to use a whip with enough ruthlessness and skill. But the bicycle was another matter. On it I became a rider of the purple sage, almost a creature with wings. It was freedom and romance and adventure. And it did exactly what you told it to do without having to be terrorized. I still like bicycles, and except for a short time when I was in politics and journalism and fancied myself to be a man of affairs, I have always owned one, and ridden it long and well. Even now, my son Andrew and I go for ten-mile rides on our mountain bikes.

If I think of the years between 1932 and 1940, when we lived on Oxen Pond Road with a wooded hill rising half a mile away, and Leary's River running almost past our door, the things most vividly remembered are the swimming holes and the woodland paths leading to them. Every muddy patch on those paths was signed with my footprints. I tasted the leaves of every species of tree and shrub, and those large enough to climb I climbed.

The pools were small and shallow, none with five feet of water, and hardly one with four. Yet each pool had its diving rock, from which you made leaps into the depths, either headfirst or bum-first, in the latter case holding your nose to keep water from being forced into your sinuses. Each pool had its separate character. The one next upriver from the bridge on Oxen Pond Road was suitable only for children of tender years. The second had a high diving rock and one spot deep enough to enter headfirst without too much danger of braining yourself. The third was small, but evenly deep. Beside it there was a sort of mud hole where someone had cut sods, and after a rain I'd seen nude boys plaster themselves with mud from neck to toe, tar babies chasing each other along the river bank before diving into the water to emerge as clean and white as peeled bananas.

A long way down-river, perhaps half a mile, was the famous Monkey's Puzzle. I never did learn why it had such a name; it was no more puzzling than any other swimming hole, just a trifle larger than the upstream pools, and with a slightly better diving rock. Still further down (could it really have been a mile?) was the big Macpherson pool, built by Harold Macpherson where the river ran through his Westerland estate, with concrete dam and spillway, open to the public because Macpherson was a wealthy old bachelor, heir of Sir Robert Bond, a former prime minister. Macpherson fancied himself as a philanthropist.

But even the Macpherson pool wasn't the end. Still further down, the river ran through a series of steadies into the upper end of Long Pond, and there, in one of the steadies, was the big pool known as Sandy Bottom, the only place where the bottom was not paved with stones. Sandy Bottom must have had a full four feet of water extending for a hundred feet or more, a pool that kids gladly walked a mile, or sometimes two or three miles, to enjoy.

There was a dress code. In the pools upriver from Leary's Bridge you could swim nude, and girls generally did not go there at all. At the Monkey's Puzzle only the very youngest ones went naked. At Macpherson's and Sandy Bottom even the babies were clothed in at least some sort of codpiece. We also swam in the big river pool at Bowring Park, where Andrew often took us on Sunday mornings. No swimmer himself, he was proud of my swimming and diving ability, which perhaps compensated somewhat for my failures on the ice.

When I was a kid Newfoundland boys never went without shirts even on the hottest summer day, but during our last years at Leary's River, going shirtless suddenly became fashionable, and practically every boy who walked to the pools left his shirt at home, or, if his mother made him take it, wore it in the back pocket of his jeans. It was a very sexist world. Few girls went swimming. The countryside in summer belonged to boys. Most girls stayed away until blueberry season, when they suddenly began to outnumber boys in the woods and on the hills.

By the time I reached my teens I was going swimming in May, and sometimes even in April. The earliest date was April 22 one year when we had a series of warm days, and the run-off heated up somewhat in the shallow riffles over the large flat rocks. I didn't stay in long, just a short dive, then perhaps half an hour lying in the sun. The warm spell was followed by a monumental snowfall, and the week after I'd been swimming I was out on my skis, ducking my head to avoid the power lines.

I was one of the first St. John's boys on skis. I bought a pair when I was twelve years old from my uncle Carl Maidment, who made them in the family cooperage at Gagetown. One of the O'Brien men on Oxen Pond Road made me a pair of poles, as it was still impossible to buy skis or poles at any store in St. John's. I skied mostly on the slopes of Mount Scio, north of Leary's River, but later at Sugar Loaf, Logy Bay, where the St. John's Hiking Club owned a lodge.

Swimming tapered off in August when the autumn gales began, though sometimes you could still swim in September. Such swimming was usually solitary, fun in its way, but lacking the intense social atmosphere of the midsummer swimming hole, where we wrestled each other while drying in the sun and matched wits in riddles and told each other the silly off-colour jokes that boys had been repeating for god-alone-knows how many generations. At least we had sense enough not to repeat them at home. By the time my own kids were in school they had become so liberated that they inflicted some of those same jokes on me. There was something to be said, after all, for the days when kids had their mouths washed out with soap.

We rarely swam in salt water (no wonder, since the east coast of Newfoundland is washed by the Labrador Current) but I did discover, at Topsail Beach, that the sea water was wonderfully buoyant, a partial compensation for its arctic chill. I even swam briefly in the sea at Carbonear, where the water is even icier than at Topsail.

That was during a rare visit away from home, when I was spending a week with Aunt Kizz. A woman who loved children, she'd asked to have me for a visit. Jim Forbes, a cousin my own age from St. John's, was there at the same time, and together with a third boy, a friend of his, we went skinny dipping right off the rock ledges behind the house.

The rocks were black, in great slabs. The water was crystal-clear and ice-green. You could dive from various heights, then catch a ledge and haul yourself back to the sun-warmed rocks. I remember it as one of the magic experiences of my youth, and I think it may have been the first time I appreciated the beauty of nude bodies.

Aunt Kizz owned a small store next door to her house, where some young relative, a granddaughter, perhaps, sold peppermint knobs and Milk Lunch biscuits and the like. The store had a stock of lozenges, a thin brittle confection flavoured with anise. I think I spent most of my "pocket money" that trip on lozenges and, to my sorrow, have never found them anywhere else, since.

A bit later, Aunt Kiziah's health began to fail. She was then forced to sell her place in Carbonear, and move to St. John's to live with relatives for the final years of her life. So one of the magic places of childhood was closed to us.

As we grew older we sometimes swam at Oxen Pond, and later still at Big Pond on the Three Pond Barrens, a lake that must have been a mile past Oxen Pond by an almost invisible woods trail through the forest and over a hill. I always did this hike barefoot, and getting there was as much fun as the actual swimming. Big Pond was indeed a beautiful lake, perhaps almost half a mile in diameter, with crystal-clear water and never a soul to share it with you except the one or two companions who had accompanied you there. Swimming across Big Pond and back was one of the more rigorous tests of endurance. The water was always cold. You could hang around nude there all day if you wanted to—my brother and I did just that and got suitably punished for our paganism by having our bums sunburned, those being the only parts of us that weren't already tanned deep brown.

In our early teens we spent much of the summer in a cabin on Purcill's Ridge, a mile or so from Big Pond, hiking back and forth to Big Pond, the berry barrens, the peat bog where bakeapples grew, and other parts of the nearby countryside. Other boys from our school, rivals, companions, even in a very minor sense lovers, sometimes stayed there with us. Some of the boys who shared that cabin must now be grandfathers, but I can think of none of them as men, much less as *old* men. In a year or two they vanished out of my life, and the segments of their lives that intersected mine are fixed forever in that time and place. They are as unchanging as Tom Sawyer and Huck Finn, though not quite so innocent.

Later, when we were finished with school, my brother and I sometimes stayed in the cabin even in winter, but it was quite unsuitable for that—no insulation, no siding, not even double walls, cracks through which snow would drift, so cold that on a frosty night water would freeze solid to the bottom of a pail. We would build roaring fires of spruce and fir in the little stove until the cabin positively danced with heat. We would take off our clothes, go out and roll in the snow, come in dripping, and towel ourselves dry beside the fire—a quick and stimulating way to take a bath.

The cabin had one room, ten feet by twelve, with a pantry walled off in a corner, a table under a window, and two single bunks on the back wall. The pantry was roofed over below the rafters, providing sleeping space for another two or three boys. A total of five could use the cabin, but usually it was two to four. My father and mother, our cousin Bob, my brother and I, built it in a single day, and got eight or nine years of great service out of it.

While living in that cabin I saw my first moccasin flowers, and marvelled that such things grew wild in Newfoundland. I saw my first pine grosbeak, too, and thought it must have escaped from a cage. I did my first serious woodcutting. My brother and I cleared out a stump field, using ropes and levers, axes and pickaxes, until we had a park-like clearing in the woods that he and his family and their friends continued to use for picnics until his death in 1994.

We learned to travel easily over glacial debris, skipping from rock to rock; we learned to walk over fields of dry reindeer moss that crunched delightfully underfoot if the sun was shining, but lay down like silk in mist or rain. Walking barefoot over the Newfoundland barrens in summer is a delight. There is always a carpet of mosses and lichens or tiny shrubs and flat sun-warmed stones. The sun in that land is never too hot. Here and there you come to a dark tarn in a patch of bog, or a small stony lake as clear as crystal, reflecting a sapphire sky. We never got hurt, never broke a bone, never hacked ourselves with an axe, never even cut a foot, beyond a mere scratch. And I suppose we developed useful skills. We certainly worked like horses clearing out the stumps and the match-stick firs that were growing among them, and this doubtless contributed to the physical strength that we enjoyed as young men.

The shack was on The Mountainside, as we called it, what is now Groves Road and has become part of Pippy Park. By the time this gets into print there will probably be a throughway, the Ring Road, passing almost over the spot where our shack was built. There we went hiking barefoot for miles and miles across the very roughest countryside, never putting on shoes from one week's end to the next. In autumn we roamed barefoot over the barrens, picking blueberries, a habit that other berrypickers considered extremely odd.

At some time between the first and fifteenth of September the Newfoundland blueberry crop comes to its peak; it is a time when a persistent picker can gather, by hand, eight or ten gallons of ripe berries in a day. The Newfoundland barrens in early autumn are truly a delight—a rock-strewn, mossy and lichen-covered wilderness, its vegetation ranging from an inch or two in height to a foot or more—an undulating heathland over which it is an endless pleasure to roam on foot in the cool sunshine. By the age of fourteen I was spending whole days alone on the barrens or in company with my brother. By our late teens, when we had learned the delights of port and Amontillado, we took to converting much of our harvest into wine, as Charlie continued to do for the rest of his life.

One of the things I missed when I moved to Nova Scotia was berry picking, roaming barefoot over the seemingly endless red and gold barrens as I had done every year from the age of fourteen until past the age of fifty, returning at sunset with a pair of four-gallon pails filled to the brim, and sometimes piled high.In the autumn of 1985, on the excuse of doing research for *The Newfoundland Rangers*, I got to St.

John's at the time of a bumper blueberry crop, spent every afternoon for several days on the barrens once again, and made fourteen gallons of blueberry wine.

As childhood merged into the teenage years my brother and I did a lot of walking. We often went to Cabot Tower, occasionally with one of our school friends, and sometimes walked over the hill to Cuckold's Cove. Freshwater Bay, on the other side of the Southside Hills, was a longer hike, but had the advantage that it was a place where you could swim before starting back for home. Blackhead Cove, beyond Freshwater Bay, seven miles from Campbell Avenue, was an even longer hike. Cape Spear was also possible, though once you'd tramped over the Southside Hills for some seven miles to Black Head, you'd hesitate to go another mile and a half to Cape Spear, and then face a nine-mile walk to your grandfather's house.

Cycling was hardly possible on such routes (it would be with today's bicycles, but we'd never seen a bike with gears) though I sometimes went by bicycle to Topsail, a run that involved only one long hill. I was forty-six years old before I owned a bicycle that would climb hills.

Our quarter-acre on Oxen Pond Road gave us space for gardens—vegetables out back, an apple tree that actually ripened apples (extra early transparents), and in front a flower garden that gave me many hours of pure delight, especially on summer evenings at dusk. With my own money I bought such popular plants as cactus dahlias from a nursery, and such exotics as ornamental thistles. But nothing gave me more pleasure than the common night-scented rockets, which grew there almost wild.

Some of my plantings succeeded, others languished; I still knew nothing about the nutritional needs of plants, the necessity of limestone for many of them, and so on. But the garden, at any rate, became a place where I could sit on a rustic bench that I had built myself and dream about being a poet while the light faded from the sky over Mount Scio, and the trees bent in wild silhouette against the pearly afterglow. It was a beginning, the first of several gardens; eventually I would learn to be a skilful gardener with shrubs, trees, flowers, vegetables and fruit; it would grow into a passion in which even the heaviest labour would be transmuted into an act of love.

I'm not sure how much food Vina produced in her garden—nothing, certainly, to compare with the year's supply of vegetables that I grew myself once I began doing it seriously. We bought quite a lot of food at the door. Throughout the thirties some small farmers peddled their produce from pickup trucks: cabbages, turnips, carrots, beets, potatoes. It must have been very cheap, for though I don't remember what the vegetables cost, I do remember what we paid for codfish sold in the same way: you could buy a large codfish at your gate for twenty cents, one weighing four or five pounds for ten cents, and a small one, perhaps a pound, for a nickel. There was no relation between the price of food and its inherent value. A pound of hamburger cost more than a large fish, and a single egg more than a small fish. You could buy cheddar cheese for fifteen cents a pound.

On the corner of Oxen Pond and Freshwater Roads, a quarter of a mile from our house, was Linegar's store, then a little place with a dingy interior and a wooden counter, kept by a wonderful old Irish woman who sold us peppermint knobs, Hershey bells, and drugs. Here, when we were old enough to be tempted by our first sinful experiments, we bought our first Irish Porter, brewed in St. John's. It came in eight-ounce bottles, just the right size for apprentice drinkers, and a perfectly innocent way to be introduced to alcohol. Here, too, we bought our first cigarettes, *one at a time*, out of an open package of Flags. Cash was so scarce that even grown men often bought one or two cigarettes instead of a pack. Here, too, I bought my first package of Bugler tobacco for twelve cents, and clumsily tried rolling my own. Later I graduated to the more luxurious brand called Target, at fifteen cents, and learned to roll with a fair degree of skill.

Smoking was not only sinful (according to most fundamentalist sects) but also bad for your health, and this was well known, even in the thirties. Cigarettes were "coffin nails." People didn't get "lung cancer," but they got "smoker's cough" and died of it anyway. Andrew told me, as soon as I was old enough to know where babies came from, that women who smoked while carrying a foetus had babies who were born underweight and sickly. Despite such knowledge, everyone got hooked, me included. We didn't really believe that tobacco was all that bad for you; we didn't really believe it until the hard statistical evidence began to come down in the fifties, and tobacco began to appear as the true killer drug, causing cancer, heart disease, emphysema, and heaven knows what else. Old Mrs, Linegar was a darling, the most innocent of drug peddlers. The age of innocence was still with us.

What sex education we got from our parents (needless to say, nothing whatever came from the school) was sketchy, fallacious, and harmful. Vina warned us what wicked and dangerous creatures girls could be. She remembered from her childhood girls she'd known who played a disgusting game called "looking at the little boys' buds." She talked about the dangers of diseases, especially syphilis, but seemed vague about how contagious it was. She told us how a man up the road had been accused of "showing off before the girls next door," but speculated that he might have been guilty of nothing worse than dressing too near a window.

Despite her awareness of what little girls did with little boys, Vina must have led a very sheltered life, because when she heard her young son use the word "fucking" one day she knew it was a "bad word" but had to ask Andrew what it meant. He was flabbergasted.

"You actually don't know? It's...well...it's the same as fornication."

"Oh." Long pause. "He picked it up in school I suppose. I won't let him say it again."

"Of course not."

Andrew wasn't quite as bad as Vina. He saw nothing wrong with kids swimming or playing in the nude, and said so, though Vina regarded it as shocking and indecent. But if it came to actually talking about the sex act, he was as tongue-tied as she. When I complained that the rooster was attacking the hens, he took me aside and tried to explain.

"You really don't know what he's doing? That's how the chickens get into the eggs. If the rooster didn't do that to the hen, there wouldn't be any germ of life inside the egg."

That was as close as he ever came to talking about sex with me until thirty years later when he told me—to my utter astonishment—about the homosexual activity of a man who rented a room from him and "played the part of a woman" with his male friends.

The explanation about the rooster wasn't very satisfactory. What I saw the rooster do was jump on the hen and grab her comb in his beak, often drawing blood as he did so. This, I assumed, was the sex act. I knew what bulls did to cows, because I saw it happening, but I was well along in adulthood before I realized that birds copulated in the same way as mammals, with organs near their tails. I had always assumed that the sex act in birds was a matter of beaks and combs.

This embarrassment on the part of our parents, this lack of frankness, at least spared us what would have been far worse—the preaching and badgering and punishment that so many children endured for being human, sexual animals. At school the boys said that masturbation made hair grow on the palms of your hands. Why they didn't all have hairy hands they never explained. At home there were no such threats. The matter was Beyond Discussion. So we escaped the hypocritical and self-righteous lectures under which so many other children suffered. Vina did, however, leave lying about a fat volume called *The Science of Life*. I read it avidly. It was not science, of course. It was nineteenth-century superstition, full of the most arrant quackery about health. But it did show drawings of sperm cells, and of foetuses in the process of development. It explained, too, the terrible dangers of what it called "self abuse," the feeble-mindedness, physical weakness, and even insanity that it caused. About the actual processes of intercourse it said nothing at all.

Chapter 7

Captain John's dabbling in history aside, you could hardly call us a literary family. Apart from newspapers and occasional magazines, our parents read nothing except religious books and tracts. The only one who read any general literature at all was Lillian, who had a few books that she treasured.

The daily press gave us our first taste of imaginative writing. We were raised from infancy on Thornton W. Burgess's bedtime stories in *The Evening Telegram*, delivered daily for one cent a copy. I remember how shocked we were when the cost increased to two cents. Later we got our daily dose of Little Bennie, a family comedy that also ran in *The Telegram*.

Then there was *The Family Herald*. Weekly we turned, excited, to its page of children's stories and easy-to-solve puzzles. We saw our favourite aunt working out its crochet patterns. We saw our father reading the lines of music, whistling the tunes from its page of Old Favourites. Later on we memorized the notes of the treble and bass clefs, as they were called in those days. It was a great shock to me, when I began reading open scores in my teens, to discover that there were other clefs than those two God-given bases of celestial harmony from which my father could spell out a tune.

Andrew had no taste or ability for anything beyond "Drink to Me Only With Thine Eyes" or "The Blue Bells of Scotland." For the latter air, which he played on the violin, I invented a fancy piano counterpoint that he absolutely loved—-something like what Bach did with "Jesu Joy of Man's Desiring," only, of course, much faster and less complex and not written by a musical genius. Vina had no musical talent at all. She learned to thump out a hymn on the piano from the notes mechanically, but she could never sing even approximately on key, though she took voice lessons and tried hard. Her sense of pitch was off by about half a tone.

The Family Herald was not much of an introduction to music, but its wide range of reading appealed to almost every rural and small-town family in British North America—its influence on a whole generation of Canadians and Newfoundlanders could hardly be over-estimated. Everyone from Harold Innes to Harold Horwood grew up on it.

In our house its influence was balanced by a marvellous collection of books called *The Pocket University*, sold to Andrew by some door-to-door book salesman. Despite the title there was not a single chapter on science, mathematics, Latin, Greek or Sanskrit. It was a straightforward literary anthology: thirty-six volumes of poetry, short stories, essays, plays and autobiography. Here I encountered Thackery's *Book of Snobs*, Kipling's *The Man Who Would Be King*, and the full range of American popular writers from Ben Franklin to Bret Hart. Prejudiced by this early diet of goodies from the American literary awakening, I have never gotten rid of my preference for American over English writers.

Some of the best of *The Pocket University* was in its two volumes of humour. My brother and I read those two books to tatters, and I still remember some of it, not so funny now as it seemed then:

> Susan Simpson strolled sedately
> Stifling sobs, suppressing sighs;
> Seeing Steven Slocum, stately,
> She stopped, showing some surprise...

and so on for three stanzas in which every word, except one preposition in the last line, started with an "s." I could quote it all, letter-perfect, but

I spare you the last eight lines in which Steven proposes, is accepted, and fathers "six small Slocums" in six seasons! Such fun!

There, too, were the purple cow, and Little Willie, and Mark Twain's jumping frog, and even Stephen Leacock doing his banking. One Little Willie that I'll never forget still seems to me excruciatingly funny:

> Willie and three other brats
> Licked up all the Rough on Rats;
> Father said, when Mother cried,
> "Never mind. They'll Die Outside"

If universities were really like this, I wouldn't mind being an academic.

I don't think Daddy Andrew (as Vina called him) read very far in *The Pocket University*, but it became the basic education of his two young sons. Later he supplied us with an eight-volume illustrated dictionary, and a twelve-volume encyclopaedia, *The Universal*. One step down from the *Britannica*, and ten steps less forbidding, it was an absolute delight that we devoured from cover to cover. From the dictionary we acquired a taste for etymology. It was fascinating to learn that a common English word had come to us from the Indo-Europeans by way of the Romans and the French, with relatives in Germany, Spain and Scandinavia.

Captain John would have approved of The Universal Encyclopaedia. His own favourite reference book was a monstrous volume of *Webster's Unabridged* with thousands of illustrations. But he would never have supplied the frivolities of *The Pocket University*. History was much more to his taste. His copy of Josephus was damaged but not destroyed in the fire. Eighteen years later I rebound it in durable cloth, and decorated the cover in coloured ink and gold. I still have it. I also rebound his Revised Version of the Bible, though I discovered that it was a pretty poor fish compared to the King James. I've owned many translations of the Bible, at least six, I believe, and the only modern one that seems to me to offer very much is Rotherham's. From it I culled the title of one of my TV documentaries—"The Roaring Deep."

The greatest literary influence of all were the Jewish prophets, as translated by King James's scholars (with a lot of help from Tyndale and others) and quoted in fluent oratory by my father:

"And the Ransomed of the Lord shall return and come to Zion with songs and everlasting joy upon their heads—they shall obtain joy and gladness, and sorrow and sighing shall flee away."

"Behold the days come, saith the Lord, that the heavens shall depart with a great noise, and the elements shall melt with fervent heat, the earth also, and the things that are therein shall be burnt up."

"They shall beat their swords into ploughshares, and their spears into pruning hooks; nation shall not lift up sword against nation, neither shall they learn war any more."

"For behold, we shall not all sleep, but we shall all be changed, in a moment, in the twinkling of an eye, at the last trump—for the trumpet shall sound, and the dead shall be raised incorruptible, and we shall be changed. For this corruptible must put on incorruption, and this mortal must put on immortality. . . and then shall come to pass the saying that is written, 'Death is swallowed up in victory.' "

I could go on quoting page after page of such lines from Amos to Paul. Half a century's traffic through my brain—Einstein and Pauling and Schopenhauer and McLuhan and Capra—has done nothing to erase the imprinted glory of that marvellous rhetoric that the Jews passed on to the English-speaking world. I have read the best translations of the Greek dramatists, and some of the Latin poets and rhetoricians. They wrote nothing at this level. No "influence" that I later encountered, not Djuna Barnes nor Flaubert nor Conrad nor Henry Miller, could exert upon me anything like the effect of those poet-scholars of the Reign of King James. It matters not in the least that the material they worked upon was a tissue of myth and superstition and wishful thinking; it is still the greatest literature in our language, and I was imprinted by it for life. Thank God, as Margaret Laurence used to stay.

With the eight-volume dictionary and the twelve-volume encyclopaedia came, free, a *Complete Works of Shakespeare* on onion skin in double columns—forbiddingly hard to read, and yet it was here, not in school, that I encountered Lady Macbeth, grand and villainous, the incredibly silly Othello, and the senile Lear. Here, too, were the delights of Shakespearean pornography—Venus and Adonis, the Passionate Pilgrim—and here were the dark splendours of the sonnets. I can still quote the half dozen great ones as though I'd read them yesterday instead of fifty years ago.

No one in our family had ever been a reader of the classics. It was virtually an accident, like a stroke of providence, that I encountered at home some of the greatest things in the English language. By the age of fourteen I was already lost forever to the abandoned life of the poet, had purchased, with money earned by milking cows and hiring out a horse, my own copy of the poetic works of Milton, and had shaken the school principal to his scholarly butt by turning in, on free assignment, a long, expository essay on *Paradise Lost*. I'm glad the essay, too, is lost. No one in our family believed in cherishing our childish precocities. Thank God again. Much better to live with the love poems I wrote at the age of eighteen and twenty than the priggish pomposities of a few years earlier. I can quote the invocation to *Paradise Lost* fully as well as I can quote the prophet Isaiah—I can't remember a single phrase that I wrote about it.

School helped out marginally. The teacher who first put me at the head of her class also discovered my taste for reading and gave me a copy of the complete works of Tennyson. I won books as prizes: *The Boy Through the Ages* that year, handsomely bound and illustrated, full of young Greeks at nude athletics, of boys in the middle ages learning to hunt with falcons, of Victorians keeping a stiff upper lip while getting caned for making mistakes at cricket. I now realize that there wasn't a lower-class boy from cover to cover—not even a young swineherd, let alone a factory hand or a chimney sweep—and all of them, of course, were Europeans, descended from Athens through Venice to Cambridge and Westminster. It was great food for the imagination, just the same.

And then, Lo!, there were classroom libraries from which you could borrow *The Dove in the Eagle's Nest, Richard Carvel, Treasure Island,* and even, perhaps, such recent bestsellers as *Greenmantle* and *Prester John.* I still wish I could write a rip-roaring adventure yarn like John Buchan, without, of course, the racism and imperialism and sexism that flavoured all his fiction.

It was my Aunt Lillian who introduced me to my first living Canadian writer—Lucy Maud Montgomery. I lapped up all her books, and identified strongly with her Emily, who filled notebooks by a candle in her bedroom. Many years later Alice Munro asked if it didn't bother me that Emily was a girl, and I began thinking about this aspect for the first time. Maybe I have to thank Montgomery for the ease with which I accepted women's equality, and the solidarity I have always felt with feminists. *Anne of Green Gables* as liberation literature; now there's a twist for you!

For a wonder, there were Canadian writers in our school books. Newfoundland had no stake in Canada—the country felt rather less friendly toward Canada than toward the United States; yet, Marjorie Pickthall, Grey Owl, Leacock, Drummond, Lampman, Pratt, and at least half a dozen other Canadians were included in our literature textbooks. I don't recall that I was particularly excited about any of them, except perhaps for Leacock and Pratt, whose work I pursued through my own reading. Pratt's rhymed epics entertained and delighted me. I bought at least five or six of Leacock's humorous books. It seemed to me that the selections made for the textbooks were not especially good ones. Pratt's "Fable of the Goats," for example, outshone "Erosion" much as Venus outshone Mercury.

Bill Blackwood, who taught me English in grade ten and eleven, was the one teacher who clearly influenced me—not my choice of career, which had been made long before, but the way I use the language. Blackwood was an English scholar with a master's from the University of Edinburgh. He loved the language, understood and enjoyed poetry, and was a purist who believed fervently that the language should be rescued from the ambient corruption of the advertisers and the slang-slingers.

It was Blackwood who taught me to not split infinitives. I still split them only after an internal debate. It was Blackwood who demonstrated the utter vulgarity of a dangling participle, the absurdity of a floating adverb, and the contemptible illogic of such phrases as "under the circumstances." I have never forgotten any of it. I still squirm when TV announcers use "hopefully" instead of "We hope that", or, even worse, announce that in the early part of her career some superstar worked "surprisingly" in a strip joint. Worse again, I see some of those with the highest reputations in Canadian literature using such ignorant constructions when writing in their own voices. I know we're a nation of slobs, but our leading writers ought to know, and to do, a little better than the illiterates who flourish on the picture tube.

Blackwood also taught me the conscious use of imagery, such fine points as the inherent superiority of a metaphor over a simile, and the subtlety of irony as compared to satire. I learned from him the elements of metrical structure, and the ways it could be used, in prose as well as in poetry, to strengthen the structure of language.

Despite such shafts of light through the prevailing murk, school was an unmitigated ordeal most of the time. I can only try to imagine what it must have been like for those who couldn't cope with the assignments. For me it was an ordeal not because the work seemed difficult, but because the whole atmosphere of the school was one of cruelty, repression, arbitrary rules enforced by punishment, and, worst of all, a pervading ethos of viciousness among the children themselves.

I'm not sure how often the strap was actually used, once we were past grade three, where it was used daily—perhaps not more than once a week or so in most classes (and Blackwood, of course, never used it at all) but the threat of it was forever present, and when it was used the offending boy was almost always brought to the front of the class to be publicly humiliated. There was no standard strap; teachers often used a two-foot or two-and-a-half-foot length of heavy harness leather capable of inflicting atrocious punishment. The fear of the strap was a permanent part of the school environment. The fear of breaking into tears, as boys often did, was perhaps greatest of all.

Boys were whipped for all the wrong reasons—assuming there are any good ones—for being noisy or insolent in class, for failing to prepare lessons, for making more than the permissable number of mistakes in their work. No boy that I recall was ever whipped for bullying, for being savage and vicious. The two class bullies in grade five both got the strap more than once, but not for attacking younger and weaker children as they regularly did—they got it for playing hookey.

In most schools, as in ours, the strap was applied only to the hands. But in the Roman Catholic schools of St, John's, those run by the Christian Brothers, boys were often strapped on their rear ends, sometimes with their pants down. In our circle such punishments were discussed almost in whispers, like racking, or hanging by the thumbs.

Bullying was accepted by the school authorities as an inevitable part of school life—boys being boys, human nature you know—and no effort was made to control it. Like so much of the prevailing savagery, it was assumed to be inborn, perhaps it was even assigned to "original sin;" I'm not sure. Even boys who were not bullies were expected to be toughs, encouraged to be selfish and competitive and ruthless. All this, totally contrary to the professed Christian beliefs of the authorities, was accepted as the natural order of things—a natural order far deeper, far more fundamental, then anything in the Mosaic Code or the Sermon on the Mount.

Boys were expected to be cruel, not only to each other, but to any wild creatures that came their way. A great deal was written in those days about the innate cruelty of children. Later I learned how false such assumptions are. Even in *our* culture many children are not cruel, and I have encountered other cultures—in Labrador for instance—where cruelty among children is rare and aberrant and almost unknown.

Boys become cruel if they come from homes where it is expected of them. My brother and I were not cruel. We abhorred cruelty in other boys, were horrified when we saw them mutilate insects, or torture frogs by blowing them up with a straw inserted through the rectum (a favourite game among some of our companions). We never in our lives pulled a wing off a fly or threw a stone at a bird.

We took part to some extent in the mild forms of hazing that went on in the school and the neighbourhood. On his birthday a boy "got the bumps," a symbolic punishment that didn't really hurt (held by arms and legs and bumped on the arse in the grass). Boys pricked each other with pins, set thumbtacks on seats; older boys might gang up on younger ones and tickle their feet or tantalize their noses with a blade of grass—there was no real cruelty in it.

Sometimes, hazing took an explicitly sexual turn—a boy might have his genitals exposed, or his pants taken off. Usually, that was as far as it went. Rarely, someone might say, "Let's give him the prickles." Then the boy might be held down while someone pricked the sensitive parts of his body with pine needles—a treatment not actually very painful, but guaranteed to make the victim nearly hysterical.

These mild tortures were never a punishment for misdeeds, but frankly a game, a sport like bear-baiting that older boys felt it their right to inflict on younger ones. And it seemed the younger ones never deeply resented such treatment. Not only did they fail by universal custom to complain to their elders; they'd invariably be back next day as though looking for more.

Bullying was not related at all to such hazing—there was no element of play in it. It was centred in deep feelings of inferiority on the part of the bully, and was always ugly, with the bully trying to inflict real terror or real pain or both on the victim. No one hung around a bully seeking his attention, except perhaps another bully; they sometimes worked in pairs. But younger boys were always flirting with the "danger" of being pounced upon by the hazers,

This whole unhealthy complex of activity seemed to belong to the kind of society that existed in and around the school. There was less of it at the summer swimming holes, still less among the large group of children I knew later in the camping community at Manuels, and none whatever among the equally large number who swarmed through my house and garden at Beachy Cove.

I never saw Innu or Inuit children fighting or bullying each other, either. On the contrary, an older child, boy or girl, invariably acted kindly and protectively toward a younger one.

In the midst of the juvenile jungles of Holloway School and Prince of Wales College a small minority of civilized teachers who loved children managed, somehow, to survive. I had three of them, out of a total of seventeen. I look back on them with affection, but even more, with compassion.

Despite such teachers (I wish I could have dedicated a book to Bill Blackwood), and despite the love I shared with two or three fellow students, I hated and despised the school I attended, and still despise it. Nothing would have induced me to revisit it, once I had escaped; nothing would have induced me to join the Guards Club or the Old Collegians, or any of the other cliques founded upon the viciousness, the sordid savagery, the waste and horror of my school days. I did run the quarter mile for the Guards team one year in the provincial track meet, but I was never a member of the club.

Partly because I hated Holloway School and Prince of Wales so thoroughly, I was determined never to allow my own children to be twisted and tortured and damaged and belittled by the school experience. I am not against school as such, only against schools where the relationship between the teachers and the taught is something other than love and respect on both sides.

I have kept watch over my children's school experiences. There are bad aspects; they pick up nasty tricks from other kids, memorize stupid jokes that ought to be pointless to them. If I had detected the kind of "schooling" that was inflicted on me I would have yanked them out of the school system instantly. But, except for Andrew's first few weeks at Waterloo, they have had really good relationships with their teachers. Leah has always gone to school entirely on her own without the slightest urging from her parents.

Andrew spent three years with the same teacher, a specialist in teaching dyslexics, who loves kids and prefers them at the age she teaches—around eight to eleven (my own favourite age, as it happens). Andrew has never had a teacher he disliked. After a brief visit to Bridgeway Academy in Wolfville he decided, on mulling it over for a week, that he wanted to go to that school. He spent three years there in a perfectly friendly relationship with his teachers.

In our late teens we began reading literature that was almost contemporary. I read all of Shaw's plays and some of Ibsen's, the novels of H.G. Wells, the essays of Aldous Huxley, some of Steinbeck's fiction, and twentieth-century French writers in translation. Before long I was discovering such rarities as Sacheverell Sitwell's wonderful, rambling meditations on European art, and the prose works of Dylan Thomas. My brother and I even read Henry Miller before his work was in print in North America.

Our education in music and art made no such progress. Except for a few choruses and arias from *The Messiah* we were hardly exposed to classical music at all as children. We had doses of Gilbert and Sullivan in high school, and there, too, I learned a few Schubert melodies and thought them wonderful, but I was in my mid-twenties before I bought my first classical records, and began to enjoy the richness of western music from Palestrina to Prokofiev. My brother, lacking my ear for harmony, never learned to enjoy it; I wonder whether he would have, had he been exposed to orchestral and choral music as a child.

Chapter 8

Apart from helping at the dairy and in the poultry houses (and my brother, later, on our uncle's pig farm), we never worked during school vacations, never ran paper routes, or had part-time jobs in neighbourhood stores. Our parents and grandparents, I suspect, had only vague plans for us; one thing was plain, though, we were not "like other people;" we were clearly raised with the concept of being different.

This produced the curious combination of being both inferior and superior to other students at school. I felt inferior because I couldn't excel at the sports that really mattered, but there was also a secret sense of superiority, of belonging to an elite who were above and beyond the common level of humanity.

This was reinforced by our never being allowed to join organizations such as the cubs and the scouts which, Andrew assured us, were among the bundles of tares gathered together for the burning during the Harvest of this Gospel Age at the end of the Present Evil World. It is true that the scouts were vaguely militaristic at that time, marching and practising drills, activities hardly suitable for the sons of a Christian pacifist. When we went camping, we went with school friends to Healey's Pond near St. Philips and camped free-lance, rather despising the scouts, who were camped next door, and who were lined up for inspection, standing at attention, while we grilled strips of bacon over our own campfire, or chased a football around a field. We also had access to a boat, a rather tub-like skiff which we could rent from its owner for ten cents an hour. Among other things, we went trout-fishing at midnight as no scout would be allowed to do.

No Newfoundlander of the 1930s would have dreamed of offering a boy a life jacket or mentioning anything as silly as "safety rules." We were expected to have sense enough not to drown ourselves or chop off our fingers with an axe. The boats were mostly so heavy that you couldn't tip them if you tried, and if you fell overboard, you'd be expected to swim.

In a sense, we were being raised like outport children rather than townies, allowed to go off on our own, expected to be able to take care of ourselves, raised for self-reliance and self-employment rather than for a slot in the city structure—such a slot as my father had found for himself because his mother hated the sea.

I'm sure it was Vina who favoured sending us off on private camping trips—she'd be rid of us for a while, and she believed in the merits of "the country." Andrew had his reservations, knowing full well that boys might teach each other such nasty tricks as mutual masturbation. And indeed it was so: one classmate of mine who camped with us had even been initiated into more advanced forms of forepleasure by a servant girl who lived in his house. Such were the routes by which the corruption of the lower classes might spread upward into the ranks of the elect.

In the outports the stratified society was simple: sharemen at the bottom, fishing masters next, merchants and captains at the top. Any girl at any level might work for her keep for a while in some stranger's house. It was easy to be upwardly mobile. In the city it was much more complex, and the structure was much more rigid. Some city groups were not easy to classify at all. A master artisan—an independent stone carver making headstones, for instance—didn't fit into the social hierarchy. It wasn't even easy, in the city, to classify the master mariners. Some of them might achieve such distinctions as the Order of the British Empire. Did they belong with the merchants and politicians? Hardly. But they didn't belong with the tradesmen, either; in a sense they stood to one side of the mercantile society with the governor at its head, the biggest merchant families in the next stratum, then five or six other ranks descending step by step to the unskilled labourers at the bottom. The world-travelling captain floated somewhere in the top half of this hierarchy, clearly above a small shop-keeper, but clearly not in a class with those lawyers who had become KCs, and might rise to the Supreme Court and even to a knighthood. This happened to Captain John's cousin, Sir William Horwood, who had gone from law to politics, and from Attorney General to Chief Justice, ranking next below the governor in protocol. He was also clearly not in the class of the *big* shop-keepers, who owned Water Street, and, with luck, might be knighted shortly before death.

Vina sometimes complained of a woman who "didn't know her place," meaning that she was unskilled in the niceties of deferentialism. This didn't mean that she was forbidden to "better herself," even in a spectacular way, by marrying her employer or her employer's son; such marriages did happen occasionally, and the woman might rise several levels in the social scale, though her working-class origins would never be forgotten, and her husband's choice of a wife would always be regarded with suspicion. The children of such a marriage would be born into their father's class of managers or lawyers or merchants and might aspire to places in the Cabinet or the Upper House or the Supreme Court, or even the select circle of Knights of the Realm.

Top-ranking outporters could, of course, move into the city structure, usually by steps involving two generations, as had happened with Sir William Horwood, who was born in the city after his father had moved from Carbonear. Sometimes it happened in one generation, straight from the bay. A young fisherman whose father had accumulated enough money and property could conceivably become a lawyer and a politician, and, with luck and skill and ruthlessness, even prime minister.

My father's long-time employer, Albert Hickman, liked to apply this story to himself. He had worked in a fishing boat out of Grand Bank, and had become prime minister for a brief term. In fact, that wasn't the whole story. It never is. There had been money in the family from the days of its "founder," Jonathan Hickman, who had been pilot in Newfoundland for Captain James Cook. The Hickmans had been well-to-do fishermen-owners, and Albert had been sent to Mount Allison University for his education. My father's prophecy of "overalls to overalls in three generations" (quoting a working-class adage that he had picked up somewhere) was wrong on several counts. Hickman had not really started his career in overalls, but as a privileged member of the monied class of the outports, and his grandsons did not go back into overalls, either. On the contrary, they were born with wealth, and continued to accumulate it long after the original fish exporting business of their grandfather was no more. Such was the myth of the "self-made man." Almost always he was the product of a family that had been scrabbling upward for a couple of generations. I can think of no single instance where a barefoot outport boy, or a slum boy from the city, became even mayor of St. John's, much less a full member of the Water Street establishment.

In school there was a kind of savage democracy. We were all treated like criminals together, and were all expected to fight and bully and brutalize each other. A boy whose father got a knighthood might be regarded with some awe for a day or two, but it soon ceased to matter. Outside the school, our friends came from our own social level; sometimes they'd be cousins, sometimes from our school classes, but always from the middle ranks of the social hierarchy. The boys we played with, the boys we camped with, were neither corner boys nor young blue-bloods from merchant families, but out of the middle ranks of the clerks and the managers. I didn't break out of this pattern until I was sixteen, and formed the first deep, romantic friendship with a neighbouring boy on Oxen Pond Road, regardless of my mother's approval or disapproval.

School became more bearable in the upper grades. Some of the teachers were just as deplorable as those in the elementary school; others might even have been called gentlemen. Two of the deplorables in particular stand out. "Killer" Curnew was a man with a temper that he barely managed to keep under control. He'd turn literally white with rage, and was known to smash a solid oak chair against a radiator. Students were physically afraid of him, though we never heard of his maiming or injuring anybody. The other was an older man, very calm and self-assured, who could belittle you with absolutely vicious sarcasm. Ike Cramm taught math, and I escaped his sarcasm because for me math was a snap, but he must have caused untold hatred, frustration and damage to self-image in others. The boys toughened themselves against this treatment by showing contempt among themselves for such teachers. He became "Old Ike" and was always referred to slightingly, never with even grudging respect. This man's two nephews taught at Prince of Wales and were very good teachers indeed.

Bill Blackwood ran what seemed like the most undisciplined, noisy and disorderly classes in the school. In spite of this—or because of it—he was outstandingly successful. Year after year, his English students scored Newfoundland's highest marks in the public examinations. It's ironic that this most successful teacher was required to retire at sixty-five, instead of remaining in the Newfoundland school system, where his combination of scholarship, skill and humanity was badly needed. After retiring, he returned to Great Britain, and promptly landed a job in the school system there.

There were privileges in the upper school in addition to a few decent teachers. There was a science lab with bunsen burners, flasks, test tubes, microscopes, and highly sensitive balances, as well as a supply of very dangerous chemicals in a locked cabinet. There was a real library, with travel books and books on science, including one that discussed contemporary models of the atom by Rutherford, Niels Bohr, Erwin Schrödinger, and others. I still marvel that a high school in Newfoundland in the 1930s possessed a book that discussed the Copenhagen interpretation of the quantum theory, and wonder who could have been responsible for its being there. I haunted that library after class, was often there at five o'clock in the afternoon when the rules said you had to be out of the building. I even discovered that you could dodge the rules, sometimes, being overlooked by the last teacher to leave, and that the school door would lock itself behind you.

Captain John died in the autumn of 1938. The last summer of his life, at the age of eighty, he made a trip to Labrador on the *S.S. Kyle*, and hunted ducks with a ten-gauge shotgun bought especially for the occasion. The women of the house called him mad, senile, an old fool. He shrugged them off, did what he wished, and spent a few days of his last year in that marvellous land of his youth where he had fished with the schooner he had built with his own hands in the days before he started taking ships to South America and the Mediterranean. He suffered a fainting spell on the coast of Labrador, returned prematurely to St. John's to consult a doctor, and was ordered into bed.

In the last few years of his life he was considerably overweight. He was now suffering kidney failure, for which in those days there was little in the way of treatment. He stayed in bed until he died, always believing he would recover in a few days.

On the last night of his life he dreamed he was captain of a ship, and that Andrew was sailing with him; the crew died, one by one, from some mysterious disease, leaving him and Andrew to manage the ship by themselves, He had barely finished telling Andrew this dream, in the morning, when his heart suddenly failed. Andrew held him, propped up in bed, while he gasped for breath, and died. My father came out of the bedroom white and shaking. He had known Captain John was going to die, but hadn't expected it so suddenly, while his mind was so clear and his ability to spin a yarn still unimpaired.

Somehow, John Horwood had communicated his strength and self-confidence to me. Long before he died, I had begun writing, had chosen it as my life work, and had begun to endure from my family the same disbelief, belittlement and incomprehension that he had endured. The only member of the family who believed writing could be anything but a hobby was my younger brother. Long before I actually encountered it, I was well prepared for the discouragements of publishers and editors and the ignorance and stupidity of "critics." After being right when my father and mother and all my uncles and aunts and cousins were dead wrong, it wasn't difficult to believe that I was right when some publisher's hack or some semi-literate reviewer or book page editor failed to understand what I had written.

I have often regretted that my grandfather would never know how he would live on in me—and not only live, but grow, and how he will, perhaps, continue to live and grow in some great-grandchild a century and more after his own time, in a world the bare outlines of which he could never have dreamed.

On the day after his death I went to his coffin, looked at his strong, calm face, and then I went home to my father's house and composed a march for my dead ancestor. No funeral march, the simple bit of music spoke of the will to overcome:

Yes. Simple and derivative, and perhaps a little childish, but I am still proud that this expression of valour was my first reaction to my grandfather's death.

Captain John had collected a small government pension in his old age. This, and Lillian's share of the profits from the dairy, was his family's entire income. With his death, Lillian was left as sole provider for herself, her mother, and her aging aunt. She coped with the financial emergency by taking boarders. It was a struggle, but she managed. So far as I know, Andrew did not contribute to his mother's and his aunt's living expenses. He had taken salary cuts during the Great Depression, and had his own family to support on his very modest income, as well as making regular payments to the Dawn Bible Students, both locally and internationally.

At about the time of my grandfather's death I began occasionally walking home with girls. My mother's preaching against sex, and the sexual segregation practised in the school, had combined to make of them almost an alien species, but there were tentative touches across the gulf—not with the girls from my school whom I never made friends with, but with neighbours. It seems amazing to me, looking back, that one of those girls actually confided to me her experiences with her first menstrual period. We walked hand in hand along Freshwater Road while she told me how frightened she'd been, how she thought she was bleeding to death the first time it happened, and how her mother had finally got around to explaining to her that this was natural, that it happened to every woman every month, and was part of God's curse on Eve in the Garden of Eden. That's how it still was, in the 1930s.

At that point I saw no real difference between the companionship of a girl and a boy, except that boys were far more accessible, and much less likely to be disapproved of by your elders. I had the same reaction, the same feelings of affection, for young members of both sexes. At the age of fifteen I had never heard of such matters as sexual orientation, bisexuality, heterosexuality. I knew that Romeo had been in love with Juliet, and that David had been in love with Jonathan, but I didn't connect those things with sex, which was something that happened in secret, and presumably by choice, between men and women when they were breeding children. Such was the shroud of secrecy wrapping life's realities in my childhood.

On the other hand, I had never suffered Freud's "childhood amnesia." I could recall my sexuality at the age of three or four with perfect clarity: frequent erections, pleasure in exhibitionism, Vina scolding me for handling my penis, and so on. By the time I went to school I had lost interest in such infantilism, but I do recall love-fantasies involving female teachers, one at seven, one at nine or ten. Those were pallid and transient affections. Between the ages of five and eleven (when I finally discovered masturbation) I was sexually and emotionally flat, unresponsive to any overtures that may have been made to me by other children or adults, concerned only with the barbaric pursuit of various games, including mock warfare.

Sex was a true discovery, not something taught by another child, a revelation, wholly secret and wholly magic, though not a secret that I failed to discuss with my brother. A little later, at twelve or thirteen or so, we shared masturbatory experiences with other boys, but only very rarely. And for me, at least, those experiences were never pleasant. I remember a companion of my own age who was obviously very delighted when he embraced me, but for me there was never a true emotional response, and the whole business seemed slightly distasteful.

Around the age of fourteen or fifteen I invented a fantasy involving a teacher and student, and another involving twin companions—doubles—but neither involved genital contact; they were *emotional* fantasies. I was already exteriorizing, creating third-party fantasies rather than first-person ones—a habit that perhaps leads to the writing of true fiction—fiction that is neither autobiography nor personal fantasy. None of this was connected with masturbation, which still seemed to be a purely physical activity, without emotional content.

The summer when I was approaching sixteen I had a brief but strong attachment to a boy of my own age, and he to me. Neighbours, we spent our days together. We shared no sexual experiences, but we might have, if the affair had lasted, because the other boy was not sexually inhibited like me. He talked about sex, speculated about it. If I lay on my belly in the grass he'd ask if I was "getting horny." The relationship blossomed and faded in five or six weeks. But I don't want to underplay the significance of it. It did not, I suppose, deserve the name of "erotic frenzy," but it was numinous with a strong sense of affirmation of each other, and it was my first prolonged attachment to anyone outside my family.

About that time Andrew and Vina decided to build a fine new house, much more imposing and pretentious than the bungalow on Oxen Pond Road. Where would they build it? Well...there must have been arguments, though we kids didn't hear them. I know they looked at land around the outskirts of the city, including a field and patch of woods on Thorburn Road, perhaps two miles north of Leary's River. I'm sure Vina would have preferred such a place, but in the end they agreed to buy a section of what had been Captain John's estate on Campbell Avenue. It was between the original bungalow, where my grandmother and aunts still lived, and the two-story house on the corner of Campbell and Cashin Avenues built by Sandy Benson, my uncle by marriage and owner of the big horse barn and forge that lay just to the north of us on Mount Pleasant Avenue, also on land purchased originally by Captain John.

Andrew planned the house we later called "140 Campbell Avenue" or just "140" for short, along lines that would have been regarded in the twenties and thirties as solidly middle-class: upstairs, five bedrooms, one for the parents, one for each child, one guest room; downstairs, a sitting room, dining room, library and kitchen. Dining and sitting rooms were joined by "French doors" so some twenty people could be accommodated in what would amount to a single room when they were opened. Both rooms had bay windows facing south, and small fireplaces designed to burn coal on their north walls. The two largish bedrooms directly above also had fireplaces. There was a full basement, coal-burning furnace, and hot-water radiators throughout the house.

Charlie and I worked full-time with the builders on "140." The work was back-breaking. We mixed concrete by hand, with shovels. Charlie also worked as a mason's helper, laying brick for the two chimneys, and mixing mortar. I worked at another gruelling task—scraping and sanding the white oak of the floors *by hand* until it was smooth enough to take a polish.

I'm sure Andrew drove lots of nails and sawed lots of boards, and I know he built the mantelpieces himself, using BC fir, a wood he always loved, for some inexplicable reason. To me it looks positively tacky. But he didn't work one quarter as hard as his two teenaged sons.

The library started out as a fair-sized room that would have housed a couple of thousand books, desks, typewriters, and so on, but was soon reduced to a cubby-hole because Vina decided she needed a "sewing room." So most of the library was partitioned off, leaving room for a small built-in desk with drawers under it, a couple of bookshelves above, and a few other shelves on two of the walls. In this cubby-hole my father worked at his radio broadcasts, religious and secular, and I wrote the first sketchy draught of the book that, forty years later, would become my third novel, *Remembering Summer*. It is a simple fact that I never at any point abandoned that book, but went back to it again and again, over a period of half a lifetime, adding, deleting, rewriting, rearranging. It became the only true Canadian "novel of the sixties," with much of what seemed to be the peculiar ethos of the sixties in it, but even when it was finally published, in 1986, it contained long passages that had been written in 1945 and 1946, just at the close of the Second World War.

Chapter 9

The two people most important to me in my early adulthood were Janet and Irving Fogwill. Insofar as I had a master and teacher who shaped the direction of my early life, it was Irving. Insofar as I had a first love among women, it was Janet. Together they altered and shaped my life as no others had done since the death of my grandfather.

Irving, twenty-two years my senior, was not a father figure. He was the senior sorcerer, my brother Charlie and I his apprentices. Janet was more to him than a wife. She was his friend and companion, partner in all his enterprises, his intellectual equal. They read the same books, played the same games, drank too much rum together, shared the same friends; never, before or since, have I encountered a more satisfactory marriage.

The fact that Janet was a Horwood, she and I third cousins or something of the sort, had nothing whatever to do with bringing us together. We met because Irving had published a slim volume of poetry that Charlie and I admired (*Prelude to Doom*, 1931). We were complete strangers, never having met until we wrote Irving a letter, telling him we had read his book, and asking if we could meet. It was his first appeal from younger writers, and the Fogwills took us to their bosoms instantly.

Irving, it turned out, was the one person in Newfoundland in touch with fully contemporary writing. He had correspondents in far places, and was familiar with names such as Djuna Barnes and Anaïs Nin, Henry Miller, Kafka, Celine. The Fogwills were also in touch with the movement that came to be known, twenty years later, as the sexual revolution, the small Bohemian subculture that existed in such far away places as New York and Los Angeles. They collected the erotic—not pornographic—literature of the period and corresponded with people who practised what would later be called orgies.

"We've lately begun to do the daisy chain," one of them reported in a letter to Irving. There was no explanation as to what the daisy chain might be, but speculating upon the possibilities was an interesting intellectual exercise.

With this kind of background, it is hardly surprising that Irving was tolerant if Janet and I flirted together a bit, if she posed for me in the nude while I sketched her near-perfect body or photographed her under a waterfall. (The pictures didn't survive long. I'm sure my mother found them and burned them, as she had a habit of doing with anything of mine that she failed to approve). Janet was a woman of remarkable vitality, palpable sex appeal, and lively personality. I'm sure I was just one of the many admirers who flocked around her in the early and middle years of her life. I can think of Janet in no other sense than as a person with more of everything than it is the lot of common people to possess—more intelligence, more wit, more sparkle, more energy. She had, with a superb body, great strength of character—too much character in her face to be "beautiful."

This was by no means a triple relationship like that of Anaïs Nin and the two Millers. It was more complex than that, and more innocent. Irving always felt he was a bit too old for Janet, and stated explicitly that he wanted her to have her fun while she was still young enough to enjoy it—always with the implicit reservation that it did not include too deep an emotional attachment on her part. How deep would be too deep? Well...that never became quite clear.

A good deal more came out of my friendship with the Fogwills than my first fascination with a mature woman, or my first acquaintance with modern writing. There were many elements—one of them being the involvement in the organized labour movement that occupied both me and my brother between 1945 and 1948. There were no pro-labour sympathies in our family. The strikes that Irving had helped to lead in the 1930s had been opposed by my parents, who considered their place to be with the managers. It was while sitting in the Fogwills' parlour sipping rum that Charlie and I came around to the view that organized labour was a cause we should support. There was no active proselytizing by the Fogwills. We simply absorbed the attitude from them. Though we were both members of the Longshoremen's Protective Union, we never took any active part in its affairs. We became labour activists because Irving had such a lifelong commitment, and through him we met such local union leaders as Ron Fahey and Bill Frampton of the Newfoundland Federation of Labour, and Jim Ryall, chairman of the St. John's Trades and Labour Council.

Charlie and I worked at the kind of jobs our father could get for us. The foreman who hired longshore workers for A.E. Hickman and Company worked directly under Andrew. So we worked on coal boats and salt boats as checkers, and once or twice at other cargo, only occasionally as labourers, and only rarely at places other than Hickman's.

It was war time. Manpower was in short supply, and long shifts were in demand. The ships sometimes worked around the clock, and then we all worked double shifts, twenty hours out of twenty-four. I remember coming off such shifts almost too exhausted to walk home, and I wonder now how middle-aged men in their forties and fifties managed to so it. They did, somehow. The foremen also resorted, now and then, to hiring boys as young as fifteen, or perhaps even younger, to work the coal boats, and teamed them up in such a way that three of them did the work of two men.

Later I worked for the Cape Company building naval installations at St. John's. I was a fully committed pacifist, as my father and uncle had been a generation earlier, and I expected to have to go to jail for pacifism before the war was over (I would never get off on medical grounds like my father). But somehow, building naval dockyards and ammunition stores didn't seem to be at all the same as fighting. When the Americans began building bases in Greenland, I wanted to go there with other construction workers from St. John's, but my father was adamantly against it. I suppose I should have been able to tell him to go take a flying so-and-so, but when it came down to a confrontation between an eighteen-year-old and a man of forty-eight, he was still the boss. So I missed Greenland, and have regretted it ever since. I worked, instead, as a carpenter's helper in St. John's. A helper, in those days, was not someone who fetched and carried, but a hammer-and-saw man. So I drove a lot of nails, and sawed a lot of boards, and did a lot of painting too, including one house on contract.

Still later I worked in a garage for my uncle, my mother's kid brother Carl. Four years my senior, more like a cousin than an uncle, he was a terror for work, drove himself with savage determination, and expected me to keep up. One evening after closing time we stayed behind, took the engine out of a car, installed it in another car, tuned it, and had the second car running properly before going home to catch forty winks around dawn. We were back at 8:30 to open up.

A little later, when the war had made it impossible to buy a new car of any kind, Carl bought two wrecks at salvage prices, one a burnt-out shell with an engine that had been destroyed in a fire, the other with a good engine but a body that had been demolished. Though they were completely different models, he made the engine fit the body, put in new glass and upholstery, spray-coated the burnt shell with three coats of paint, drove his hybrid for almost a year, then sold it for $4,500, about twice what it would have cost new, before the war.

The pace at the garage was so killing that I quit, but Carl talked me into going back. I was still there after he moved on. I worked briefly for the man who had been his partner, but when I got involved in labour politics, he told me I'd either have to drop the politics or the job, so of course I dropped the job, and within a year I was working full-time as a labour organizer. Labour and labour politics continued to be my full-time occupation until I joined Joe Smallwood's Confederate campaign in 1948.

Irving had talked my brother and me into becoming socialists, of a sort. Through him we met the men who were then organizing the St, John's District Labour Party—Jim Ryall, Ron Fahey, Billy Bond Taylor, Bill Frampton, and others. We rushed into this absorbing work with great gusto. Within a week or so I was writing speeches, canvassing the newspapers for advertising space, making my own appeals to the voters on the radio, and introducing candidates for councillor and mayor.

We elected none of our candidates, but got a very tight labour vote, all of our people barely missing election, grouped together immediately below the six who got in. With the election for the national convention a few months later, we decided to run candidates in all six St. John's seats, and elected two of them. One of our elected candidates, Gordon Higgins, later became chief spokesman for Newfoundland in the House of Commons. One of those defeated, Phil Forsey, became a minister in the first provincial government.

That, however, was the end of the Labour Party. It simply foundered on the issue of Confederation, an issue on which it was impossible for any political party to unite, at that time. To illustrate: the two Fogwills, my brother and I, Taylor and Frampton, all worked avidly for the Newfoundland Confederate Association. Ryall and Fahey opposed it just as vigorously. Our two elected candidates also opposed Confederation. Labour did not venture again into Newfoundland politics in any organized way until forced to do so by the Smallwood government in 1959.

Like so much that happened to me in my youth, becoming a leader of organized labour seemed entirely accidental, I was walking to the old Gosling Memorial Library on Duckworth Street one evening, and as I was approaching the Anglican Cathedral I heard a voice hollering "Hey, Harold, hey, come over here a minute!" It was Jim Ryall, then chairman of the St. John's Trades and Labour Council, whom I'd gotten to know well in the Labour Party. He was standing in the doorway of Victoria Hall.

"Come in," he said, "come in. I've got a meeting of construction labourers in here—thirty or forty of them; they want to form a union. Come in and talk to them."

"I don't know anything about unions Jim," I said. "I've been to about two meetings of the LSPU in my life, and that's all."

"They don't know anything about unions, either," he said. "Just come in and give them a pep talk."

"Well...." By this time I was a popular debater, trained in the Methodist College Literary Institute. I'd talked on radio, too, and had written speeches full of Fabian socialism. It was no use saying I couldn't speak.

So I went upstairs with Jim to the small gathering of construction labourers. I told them how you could break one stick, but not a bundle of sticks tied together. I told them how the workers of the world were uniting to demand their fair share from the greedy capitalists. I explained how great oaks can grow from little acorns, how this small nucleus could grow into a powerful organization. When I sat down they roared their applause, and demanded that I become their chairman. What could I do? I told them to go and spread the word among their fellow workers on the construction sites, and promised to meet them two weeks hence for our first big organization meeting.

I began visiting the construction sites myself (there was massive post-war building underway) and soon met a man working as foreman for the St. John's Housing Corporation, a man old enough to be my father, strong enough to tie me in a knot, powerful, level-headed, instinctively trusted by everyone who worked under him. This was Jack White, who promptly switched his allegiance from his employer to the new union, and was the major force in an organizing campaign such as St. John's had never seen before.

A few days before the second meeting of our new union, Jack said to me, "You'd better hire the Longshoremen's Hall. It's the only place big enough for the crowd we're going to get." I was doubtful, but hired the hall anyway. And it wasn't big enough. The crowd overflowed the hall and stood outside on the steps. There was little need for oratory. They were there to sign up, to pay their dollar and take their membership cards. In a matter of weeks we had the largest local union in St. John's, with more than two thousand members.

And we had what was certainly the most powerful executive committee of any union in Newfoundland—I believe the most powerful that has ever existed, from that day to this. What other union ever had a secretary who was reading Kant and a chairman who was reading Heisenberg? Besides Jack White, as delegate, and my brother, as secretary, we had Jack Lewis, as vice-chairman, and Harry Constantine as treasurer. Lewis later became a successful small manufacturer, and Constantine became an accountant. In addition to the five officers, we had on the executive Jack Fitzgerald, Clarence Harding and Angus Caines, any one of whom could have filled the chairman's job perfectly well. Every one of us had brains, ability and energy. Our interests ranged over a broad spectrum of the economy, and we were soon recruiting members from several small unorganized trades: cement finishers, plasterers, truck drivers, bus drivers, brewery workers.

Jim Ryall, who had started it all with a small push, was a bit dismayed. "They should have unions of their own, Harold," he insisted. "You can't have a union of everybody from priests to prostitutes." We were then on the point of organizing the cleaning women. We were chartered directly by the Newfoundland Federation of Labour, not by one of the internationals, and saw no reason why we couldn't have a wide-ranging industrial union of just about everybody. Ryall, like the other members of his Council, was from one of the international craft unions. Their aim was betterment of the individual within the craft structure. Our aim, like that of most large industrial unions, was social revolution, the betterment of the whole class of people at the bottom of the economy.

In time, we spawned some locals. In time, too, I was hired first by the Newfoundland Federation of Labour, and then by the Canadian Congress of Labour, to organize Newfoundland workers. Among "my" unions was a separate union of plasterers, a separate union of painters, a union of fishermen and fish plant workers at Burin, and another union of general workers at the American base in Argentia. White, without my assistance, organized the brewery workers and the St. John's bus drivers, who, for some reason, were not part of the strong pre-existing Municipal Workers Union. In effect, we were tying up all the loose ends in eastern Newfoundland. On the eve of Confederation the work force—with the sole exception of public employees—was almost one hundred percent organized, and worked under contractual agreements with their employers. We had, by then, a more solidly organized work force than any province of Canada.

The labour interlude was a ball. Pure fun and games. Revolution in the 1940s. Talk about lost causes! Though I had a close association with some Canadian communists, they knew enough not to trust me. I regarded two or three (Bert Mead of Vancouver, A.A. McLeod of Toronto) as personal friends. But how right they were not to trust me! No one with my urge for personal freedom and fulfilment could ever be a communist. They shouldn't have trusted themselves, either, as it turned out. When it came down to issues like the invasion of Hungary and Czechoslovakia, damned few of them were able to preserve their communist faith. So much for those pedestrians of the Old Left. Though they may have been mistaken in their loyalties, and in their willingness to change them, they were damned fine and dedicated people, some of them, with an almost saint-like willingness to spend themselves for the common good.

When I was campaign manager for the St. John's District Labour Party I was still too young to vote, but reached the age of twenty-one just before the election for the national convention, and voted in the next seven or eight local, provincial, and federal elections. Later, disillusioned with politics, I often didn't bother to go to the polls to choose between candidates who were all totally unfit to govern. But there you are—those are the people we allow to run the country, people who should never be given any kind of public trust.

The organizing was a ball, too, night after night in the dirty little halls in the slums, rooms reeking of dead tobacco smoke—rooms which I still revisit in my dreams—talking with construction workers, truck drivers, cement finishers, painters, plasterers, gas shed workers, brewery workers. Imagine those men in their forties and fifties and sixties trusting a bourgeois kid of twenty and electing him head of their organization! The General Workers Union, after Confederation, was carved up by the Canadian Trades and Labour Congress into locals of the Teamsters, Hod Carriers, and so on. Some fate! They destroyed a powerful organization, and played straight into the hands of the capitalists.

We had the tightest discipline of any union I'd ever heard of. We invented—or reinvented—the rotating strike and used it with deadly effect. Not only had we never heard of it; the employers we dealt with hadn't, either, and were convinced that anything so devilish must have been devised in Russia for the destruction of the free world economy. In fact, I had dreamed it up myself. You had to have a tight union to use it properly, and we did have a tight union. All that was ever needed was a wave of the hand, and every labourer and minor tradesman on a construction job would drop his tools and follow you out to the street.

Soon the trades were joining us—not as members of our union, of course—they had their own unions—but in the larger association that we called the Building Trades Council, of which I became president, and of which Jack White was general business agent. This council of all construction workers, skilled and unskilled, became so powerful that in the end we practically controlled the industry and dictated working conditions. We raised all wages in the industry substantially, but we raised those at the bottom by three hundred percent in three years. Not a revolution, exactly, but something quite unprecedented.

I was a power-tripper for a while. I loved the picket lines. I enjoyed having men follow me. I enjoyed meeting employers' committees, knowing that they respected me, feared me a little, knowing that in the matter of brain power I was superior to any of them, and had the means to deal with them effectively.

We knew how to use psychology, too. Once when we were on strike in the spring, and thousands of young trees were heeled in at Churchill Park (then being built by the St. John's Housing Corporation), their buds about to burst, planting time already past, we offered to go back to work temporarily, just to plant the trees and save them from dying. This so impressed Judge Brian Dunfield, the corporation chairman, that he quickly influenced his colleagues to settle the strike in our favour.

I became a skilled and patient negotiator. A few years later, when I was a member of the legislature, the International Brotherhood of Electrical Workers nominated me to a conciliation board. We spent many long sessions over the bargaining table, and in the end we did what no one thought possible; we came up with an agreement. The union rewarded me with my first leather briefcase, suitably engraved. The employers' committee came to me in a body, shook hands, and assured me that I had personally saved them from a lengthy strike. But this wasn't the first time I had saved employers from their own short-sightedness. A couple of years earlier, when we had forced the Newfoundland Gas Company to reorganize its shifts and raise its wages, and had been called communists for our trouble, production went up, costs per unit of gas dropped considerably, and a company that had been dying on its feet began to show a profit.

One of the interesting things to come out of the association between Charlie and me and the Fogwills was the little magazine, *Protocol*. Charlie was more a venturer than I when it came to literature. He wrote off to the Gotham Book Mart for their catalogues, and we began buying such books as *Nightwood* by Djuna Barnes and *Portrait of the Artist as a Young Dog* by Dylan Thomas. Charlie discovered Yeats, and bought his collected works. Irving supplied us with *Ryder* by Barnes, perhaps the rarest book on my bookshelf today. I was as fascinated by her work as by the first works of Henry Miller. Irving had received part of *Tropic of Cancer* from Raymond Souster in mimeograph long before it was available in print in North America,

If any one book, near the beginning of my career, had an enormous influence on me, it was that one. It burst like a bombshell among the avant garde writers of the late 1940s, and its influence continued to spread until it had transformed the literature of the western world. We had our first introduction to Henry Miller in 1946. Published in Paris, he was banned from circulation throughout the English-speaking world. Fortunately, Souster and one or two colleagues of his were issuing a magazine on mimeographed foolscap from such unlikely places as Cape Ray in Newfoundland and Cape Breton Island. Our copies were passed from hand to hand in St, John's, and read to tatters by the *Protocol* group, of which Irving and Janet, Charlie and I were the principal members, with Dave Pitt, Phil Forsey, Mike Harrington, Greg Power, and others.

When I discovered Miller, he was busy transforming the art of literature, his prose armed with the lightnings and thunders of the Hebrew prophets, but dealing with the twentieth century. Not only did Miller discard completely the cant and hypocrisy that had clothed most English literature up to that time; not only did he treat sex as one of the everyday affairs of life, without the old taboos, and, just as important, without the mystifications that had been woven around it by D.H. Lawrence, but he did it in language that fairly danced and leapt off the page.

Miller's use of language was his greatest strength. He could make it perform miracles. He made no distinction between prose and poetry, or between fiction and non-fiction; all the old categories simply disappeared in language that flowed like glowing lava from an erupting volcano.

Many years later, when Margaret Laurence and I had become close friends, she said to me: "Harold, of all the influences during my early career as a writer, Henry Miller and the *Tropic* books were far and away the greatest. His work was a revelation. Here was true liberation literature. And he didn't *write down*. He *loved* those dreadful old prostitutes that he met on the Paris streets."

Henry Miller is a writer's writer, admired, read and absorbed by nearly everyone in the literary community in the western world. Never achieving the public recognition of Faulkner and Hemingway, he has had a greater influence than both. Many of his admirers were angry because he was never offered the Nobel prize. My own feeling is that it would have demeaned him. He was an elemental force, not a literary craftsman like Steinbeck and Faulkner and Hemingway, and a greater wielder of sheer literary magic than all of them.

As it happened, Irving was the only person in Newfoundland through whom a young writer could get in touch with the leading edge of literature in English. It was a miracle that he existed at all in such a place at such a time. He provided us with exactly the kind of education we needed to balance our readings of the philosophers and scientists—education such as no university in Newfoundland or Canada was equipped to provide.

Our more orthodox studies included the German idealists. Charlie read Kant. I read Schopenhauer, Spinoza and *The English Philosophers from Bacon to Mill* (for whom I cared very little). We both read Nietzsche with avid delight.

Among our purchases from The Gotham Book Mart was a fat volume titled *The Little Magazine* outlining the history of the literary press in the twentieth century in England, France and the United States It was a revelation. Why not have our own magazine, printed in our own shop, circulated among the avant garde groups in other parts of the English speaking world?

We bought a tiny and ancient press of unorthodox construction which happened to be exactly right for what we proposed to do, A multigraph with a rotary drum, it was slotted to accept hand-set type of a special kind. You set the type from a sloping type-holder, from which it slid, one character at a time, into a type stick where you could justify it by adding thin spacers. From the type stick it was fed a line at a time into the slots of the drum. It had all the advantages of regular hand-set type, but was much faster to set up. We were limited to printing one page at a time, but this was no hardship for a magazine with a circulation between 100 and 200 copies. We quickly got the hang of it, and turned out beautiful copy on high-calendared paper. We managed to print our own covers in red or black ink dusted with gilt for a rather sumptuous effect. The copies, of course, had to be stapled and cut by hand, but we had an effective cutter. It was all great fun, and we had a product that stood up well among the little magazines of North America, few of which were so well turned out at such amazingly small cost.

Soon we had correspondents in Belgium, India, Australia, Canada, the United States and Britain. We published mainly our own work, but some, too, from foreign countries. *Protocol* was listed by the Canadian government as one of the "ten cultural publications of Canada" at a time when Newfoundland was not part of Canada at all, but a foreign country. It was the first real cultural publication of Newfoundland, and it was a bit of a shock to the few people who bought it in the bookstore at St. John's.

Because we seemed to need some serious criticism in the magazine, as well as poetry and fiction, I began writing critical articles and reviews. Among the articles were "Djuna Barnes and the Sense of Cosmos" and "André Malreaux and the Dance of Death." Among those who read them and were suitably astonished was Robert Weaver, then writing for *Northern Review* in Montreal, later to be literary panjandrum of the CBC. When I met him, some twenty-five years after *Protocol* had been abandoned, we were on a Canada Council jury, and he recalled those articles: "I remember saying at the time, 'My God, this stuff can't be coming out of a Newfoundland outport!'" And it certainly wouldn't have been, except for the Fogwills.

Protocol appeared in 1946 and died in 1948 with its last issue still on the press (one or two fragments of the unpublished last issue still exist). It was a victim of politics, not of flagging interest among its editors. Charlie and Irving, as well as I, had become so wrapped up, so totally involved in the campaign to bring Newfoundland into Confederation, that the magazine simply languished, and was eventually abandoned in the rush. There is a limit to how many things you can do in one lifetime. Music was another hobby I was forced to abandon.

I was not yet writing fiction. Poetry and essays were my vocation. Unlike the others, I had read Sacheverell Sitwell, and was deeply influenced by the way he and Aldous Huxley handled the essay. I set out to write in a similar style, and almost did. Eventually I achieved a kind of cross between Sitwell and Miller with elements of Djuna Barnes thrown in. I'd never tried writing criticism until *Protocol* appeared to need a critical article. Then, in quick succession I wrote "Djuna Barnes and the Sense of Cosmos," "André Malreaux and the Dance of Death," "E.J. Pratt and William Blake" (the last in *Dalhousie Review*).

This went so far that I began making notes for a commentary on Blake's prophetic symbolism (I still think I could have shown Norrie Fry a few things on this head.) All I needed was an English degree (absurdly easy to get) and I might have been launched on a brilliant academic career. Thank god again! I steered or was steered away from such a course—even without the degree I would have found it absurdly easy to storm the topless towers of academia.

Charlie and I read a good deal of European writing in translation—the poetry of St. John Perce, the plays of Ibsen, the horrors created by the nightmare mind of Kafka. We were deeply impressed by *The Seven Who Were Hanged, Man's Fate, Invitation to a Beheading*, and even, I'm afraid, that now-forgotten shocker, *Out of the Night*.

I was the only one in our circle who read any of Virginia Woolf. Her fiction (especially *The Waves*) struck me as boring, precious, and untrue—a judgment I stand by to this day. Apart from its preciousness, it is also sick literature. What's wrong with sick literature? Everything. Those self-pitying wails of Sylvia Plath do not really deserve to be read, no matter how truthfully they may express her death wish.

Irving tended to remain abreast of what was coming out in America. He read *City of Night, The World of O, Last Exit to Brooklyn, The Man With the Golden Arm* as they came out. I never read any of those books. On the other hand, I read the full, extended text of *The Golden Bough*, and all the translated works of Pierre Teilhard de Chardin. I even went to the length of reading some of his essays in French, a language I could only "spell out" with much labour. I read some of the literature of Buddhism, Taoism and Vedanta. I knew what was happening in science. I read most of Sartre, and was not deeply impressed, either by his fiction or his philosophy. Camus I enjoyed, also *Our Lady of the Flowers* and *Miracle of the Rose*. Génet may have been just as sick as Plath, but he was sick with life, not death. Among the modern philosophers who impressed me favourably were Nikolai Berdyaev and Martin Buber.

I read everything written by Faulkner, and to back it up, everything written by Conrad. This great artist of the early twentieth century became my principal connection to the past of the English novel. Except for Melville and a few isolated works (one by Henry James, one by Hawthorne, one by Samuel Butler, etc.) I never read the novels of the nineteenth century. I suspect that they were completed in Conrad, and that I really do not need to read Fielding. Conrad's contemporaries, Lawrence and Joyce, laid the foundations for the fiction of this century. Without having absorbed them, directly or indirectly, no one could write a twentieth-century novel. The same, I am convinced, could not be said of Fielding or Austen or Henry James. Needless to say, I was more impressed by William James than by Henry.

Michael Harrington was one of the young writers who met with Irving and Charlie and me to drink wine and discuss poetry. David Pitt was another. They both wrote poetry, but neither of them contributed to *Protocol* or continued as poets. Harrington, after a brief fling in politics and freelance broadcasting, settled into a lifetime as editor of the St. John's *Evening Telegram*. Pitt went off to university on the mainland, and later returned to Memorial University as a professor of English. He eventually became E.J. Pratt's biographer. When I met him in 1986 for the first time in many, many years, he said to me, "You warned me, when I went off to study English at university, that it would be the end of me as a writer—and indeed it was."

The occasion on which we met was the publication of my seventeenth book. Of all that group, I was the only one who really survived as a writer. Why? I don't know. Something in my character. Certainly it was not because I could write better than the others.

It was a short step into politics. Joe Smallwood came to town in 1946 looking for supporters, and since I had become a meteoric power in the land, I was one of the first to be wooed. He struck me instantly as a winner. I was converted to Smallwood himself first, and only later to his cause, not because of any political or idealistic considerations, but solely because of the economic good that would accrue to Newfoundlanders through their political union with Canada.

The Confederate campaign was, of course, an endless grind of working thirteen to sixteen hours, seven days a week. Near the end of the campaign I made my first small-plane flights, in a Norseman, to the outports and to Corner Brook, to speak on platforms. I was an excellent speaker, fluent and imagistic. Smallwood loved my oratory and envied it, as he envied Bill Keough's. He was a far more effective speaker than either of us, but when we got carried away with our own oratory on a platform, we could turn on flights of imagery that made the hair crawl up his neck.

There is no need for me to discuss Smallwood and my association with him at any length, since I've written his biography. Four years after my first steps into politics I'd dropped it all like a snake shedding its skin, and went out to get my first "steady" job. I'd worked as longshoreman, construction labourer, grease monkey; I'd published a magazine, written poetry and literary criticism and my first short story; I'd organized and led labour unions. And here I was, coming in at 8:00 or 8:30 a.m. to pound a typewriter every day on the city desk. Harold Horwood, almost a legend already, now news hound heading swiftly for the top of the journalistic heap. Not a very big heap to reach the top of, and it took me only three years to get there: star reporter, star columnist, editor of the editorial page. To everyone's astonishment, I demonstrated that people would buy a newspaper just to read a daily column. Thousands of people read "Political Notebook" and the comics, and nothing else in the daily press. At least, that's what they said in the surveys. The column had such a high rating that the Herders, owners of the paper, refused to show me the figures. Political Notebook was not just a column of political criticism. Far more, it was a column of political revelation, investigative journalism that drove the politicians in the government, and Smallwood in particular, to a state of near frenzy. Joey was almost ready to hire a hit man to get rid of me, as he admitted in an interview many years later. The Herders thought I was the greatest thing that had ever happened. But in time I grew thoroughly bored with it all. There was nowhere for me to go from the editorial desk—only the gold watch thirty years down the road.

After all the dazzle and the glory and the easy money, the new cars and the power boats, summer vacations in Labrador and winter vacations in the tropics, it was still just childhood coming to an end. I didn't even begin to reach maturity until I put all this, too, behind me, and headed for the woods, with oil lamps, linoleum-covered tables, a wood-burning kitchen stove, and the beginnings of contemplation. That was when I began the self-discovery that continued for many years in my journal, and the conclusions that began to emerge in my novels and short stories and other prose writings.

Besides the useful time I spent with the Fogwills, I wasted some time with them too—much more than I should have. They taught me to play hearts, and then contract bridge. Almost before I knew it, I was addicted to this complex, clever, and time-wasting game. A few years after I first knew them, Doreen Gill and I used to play regularly against Janet and Irving. After Doreen married, Gary Forsey and I sometimes played as partners against the Fogwills, and later against all-comers in the first Newfoundland Duplicate Bridge Club. In one memorable tournament I bid us into a grand slam, and Gary made the contract—the only partnership in the club that did it. If you want to waste time, bridge has a lot going for it. Now, I rather wish that I had been reading Fielding, or even Henry James instead.

Harold Horwood, aged two. This fancy hand-powered sled was the author's prized possession as a small child. Note the seat belt! In the background is the "tin house" dating from before 1920, and now housing Walsh's Grocery.

The three Horwood children, Ruth, Charles abd Harold, picking and eating home-grown transparents, early apples that will ripen, in St. John's. Oxen Pond Road, 1937

Fishing and skinny dipping at Leary's River, where the author learned to swim and fish. This beautiful stream was buried in a storm sewer underneath the Avalon Mall.

Cpt. John Horwood, grandfather. Andrew Horwood, father Vina Maidment Horwood, mother. Harold in 1966, year of his first book.

Executive of the General Workers Union. Standing: Bert Fitzgerald, Clarence Harding, Angus Caines. Seated: Jack White, Jack Lewis, Harold Horwood (chairman), Charles Horwood (secretary), Harry Constantine. Two of this remarkable group became accountants, two became writers, one became a prominent civil servant, and one a successful businessman. "No union ever had a stronger negotiating committee," Horwood avers.

Courtesy City of St. John's Archives

A small "corner store" of the sort that did most of the local business in the 1920s and '30s.

Courtesy City of St. John's Archives

A bit larger, but essentially the same sort of business. "Braces" of partridge (ptarmigan), "braces" of rabbits (varying hares), and shore cured fish always hung outside.

A road in the east end, shared by dogs, children and adults. In good weather the streets were always thronged with people.

Children leading a cow and calf along a St. John's road, *circa* 1930. The author led such cattle to pasture along Campbell Avenue and milked them in a barn at the junction of Campbell, St. Claire, and Mount Pleasant Avenues, now a crowded city intersection.

A cooper working in a St. John's cooperage. There were scores of such small manufacturing businesses all over the city in the author's youth.

Horses hauling firewood, helped along by sails, on Quidi Vidi Lake. Such catamarans were often hauled by dogs and pushed by their owners. During the 1930s, hundreds of city households contrived to cut their own fuel in the suburbs.

Chipping ice from a fishing ship in St. John's harbour. Icing, caused by blowing spray in storm conditions, was the gravest danger faced by ships in winter. They sometimes turned over and vanished without a trace.

Getting trap skiffs ready for the fishing season, at "Maggoty Cove" in St. John's harbour. In those days St. John's was sometimes called "the biggest outport of them all."

Spanish and Portugese fishing fleets crowded the harbour, spring and autumn, from the Sixteenth to the Nineteenth Century. The author took this photograph while working for *The Evening Telegram.*

Courtesy City of St. John's Archives

Making fish on a flake at Quidi Vidi village, a section of the city that remained a fishing outport when the rest of St. John's moved on to other endeavours.

Courtesy City of St. John's Archives

Alcock and Brown's aircraft surrounded by spectators at Lester's field, St. John's, June 14, 1919, preparing for the first successful crossing of the Atlantic by plane. The pioneer flights from St. John's and Harbour Grace created tremendous excitement and enthusiasm.

Courtesy City of St. John's Archives

The horse meets the street railway. One of the early models of electric street car stops at the end of the line, Water Street West. The light, four-wheeled delivery cart continued in use by small retailers until after the Second World War.

Photographs and drawings not otherwise identified are by members of the Horwood family.

Chapter 10

Besides Irving and Janet Fogwill I had another great friend in my youth, a man close to my own age, and aside from my brother Charles, the first true intellectual I had ever met. Irving was well-read and highly intelligent, but not an intellectual. Neither Kant nor the quantum theory nor the Tao-te-Ching came within the ambit of his far-ranging mind.

I was perhaps eighteen years old when I met Charlie Halfyard, and formed the one major intellectual companionship of my life. My relationship with Halfyard was quite different from that with any of my other friends. It had a quality of immersion. We plunged, together, into the accumulated thought of humanity. It would not be fair to Halfyard's memory to write of him in emotional terms. He was a sensitive intellectual, a late Victorian romantic, but an intellectual first and last. Our companionship was of the mind. We shared almost no other interest.

Charlie was so frail as to be a semi-invalid. He'd had rheumatic fever as a child, leaving him with leaky heart valves. He could walk only at a stroll, with effort. If he climbed a hill or a long flight of stairs, he would have to pause several times for breath. He was thin to emaciation, but his lungs and heart still had to labour to keep his reduced body going at its reduced pace.

He was a little older than I—three years, perhaps—and had pursued his private studies in a more orthodox way. He introduced me to Verlaine and Flaubert, and to such English writers as Berkeley and Hazlitt.

We both played the piano. I had taken lessons for a year or two. He had taught himself with the aid of a correspondence course. He gave me the complete course which he had used, and from it I became not only a more efficient dabbler than I had been previously, but I also began to develop a taste for such composers as Mendelssohn, Schumann, Schubert and Chopin. I became fairly adept without that quality of "touch" that marks a real pianist. It was only much later, listening to myself on tape, that I realized how bad I really was. I could hit nearly all the right keys, even in difficult passages, but I sounded like a caricature of a performer: there was no way I was ever going to learn the subtle dynamics of the keyboard that separates a performer from a hack. And yet, I had an excellent ear, with a perfect sense of pitch and timing. It was the same kind of trouble I'd had with the violin: I could never learn to control the bow properly.

Charlie Halfyard lived with his mother in what was then the country, north of St John's near the place where Leary's River flows through the Sand Pits into Long Pond, where the university campus is now. Despite his physical weakness, we used to walk for considerable distances through fields and woods and along the shore of the lake, but we were in no sense nature students; we were philosophers strolling in the country, oblivious, or nearly so, to the living world that breathed and fermented around us. My interest in the patterns of life was awakened by another older friend, much later. In the years I strolled through the fields beside Long Pond with Charles Halfyard, the living world was just the sun on our backs and the grass under our feet and perhaps a half-heard bird song from the unnoticed trees.

The most far-out thing Halfyard and I did together was deciding to learn Greek. I had learned high-school French, of course, and had taken one year of Latin, but compared to such languages Greek had a true aura of scholarship and romance about it. It also seemed to be a justifiable indulgence since at the time we both regarded ourselves as Christians. Biblical scholars, along with other scholars, were people to be admired.

We tackled Biblical Greek with the help of a first-year grammar, a Greek-English dictionary, and a Greek New Testament. We never did learn grammar worth a damn, but we quickly learned to transliterate, and picked up a vocabulary that permitted us to spell out New Testament Greek without being able to compose a grammatical sentence on our own.

With the help of scholarly lexicons that discussed the nuances of words that had split theologians into warring factions throughout the centuries, we plunged into one of the more intricate mazes of Biblical literature, and made a new translation of the Gospel of St. John. This, in turn, led us to the Greek sophists—in translation. It was Halfyard who persuaded me to read Plato, and, at a considerable remove in time and method, Spinoza. All this classical dabbling seemed to lead nowhere. I'm not sure it wasn't the greatest waste of time in my life, even though it must have been sandwiched in between sessions with Fogwill and the Labour Party, work on the waterfront, and heaven only knows how many other activities. Did I ever sleep in those years?

Again it was much later—a decade or so—before I came to the Christian mystics, and, far more important, to the Bhavagad-Gita, the Buddhist sutras, Alan Watts, and the revelation of Zen.

There has never been a parallel in my life to the mature and equal friendship I shared with Halfyard. The nearest, perhaps, has been my long-standing and richly productive companionship with Farley Mowat. But Farley, and I say this with all due deference and respect for Canada's ablest writer, is not an intellectual, just as Margaret Laurence was not an intellectual. I could never sit down (or stroll in the fields) and discuss with either of those dear friends and fellow workers the ultimate nature of matter, the space-time continuum, or the identity of the *atman* of the self and the universe, as I could discuss such things with Halfyard.

In the late summer of 1945 I was visiting my cousin Bob at Bonavista, where he was holding a summer school for student teachers who needed additional credits. He invited me to address his classes, and showed obvious pride in the images that I conjured for their edification. The school ended, and I stayed for another week, early in August. That was the week that Halfyard died.

In my absence he had contracted pneumonia. It was treated in hospital with sulfa drugs, for the true antibiotics were not yet in use, and the sulfas, despite their danger, were the "wonder drugs" of the time, prescribed for almost everything. Charlie, frail by nature, was killed by the drugs. My brother Charles wrote to me, quoting Omar's quatrain:

> For some we loved, the loveliest and the best
> That from his vintage rolling time hath pressed,
> Have drunk their cup a round or two before,
> And one by one crept silently to rest.

There must have been some other hint in the letter that he was talking about Halfyard, for though my brother was allusive and elliptical, he wasn't usually *that* obscure, but whatever it was, I missed it. I returned from Bonavista a day or two later to face a double-barrelled shocker: Charlie Halfyard was not only dead, but buried; the Americans had dropped the atomic bomb on Hiroshima.

It is difficult to comprehend, now, the shock of that first atomic explosion to people who understood atomic theory and knew that something of the kind was likely to happen, sooner or later. My brother and I were all too well aware of the possibility of the doomsday weapon, but had received no clue that it was being developed. Hard, now, to comprehend the abyss that opened beneath the feet of the cognoscenti when Hiroshima was destroyed. All in a moment, the universe was no longer man's home, but a place he shared with the dragon of the apocalypse. The only analogy I can imagine today would be a joint announcement from Washington and Moscow that a spaceship from an alien civilization was in orbit about the earth. The end of the war in the Pacific was, by comparison, an event almost too trivial to notice.

The Bomb—and the enormously escalated horror released later at Bikini Atoll—dominated, well-nigh crushed, human thought and the human imagination for the next ten years and more. That the human species might actually survive into the twenty-first century without first bombing itself back into the Stone Age seemed, at the time, a forlorn hope. I signed all the ban-the-bomb petitions. I backed causes supported by the Communists (the only people in North America, in those days, working for peace). The Soviet Union had passed a law making it a crime to publish propaganda claiming war was either desirable or inevitable; public men in the west were showered with wealth and honour for making such claims. We in the western world seemed bent on suicide, and on taking the whole world down with us. Our only hope seemed to be that Joseph Stalin (god help us!) might be saner than the likes of Truman and Eisenhower.

I began to feel by the early fifties that our most realistic hope was for a general war immediately, while some pockets of civilization might survive. I'm glad I never expressed such a view publicly, though I had plenty of opportunities. I suppose I always felt there was an outside chance we might learn to live with and control the technology of total destruction. Despite the contingency plans for the end of the world, despite the ample ability of not one, but two, hostile nations to wipe humanity from the face of the earth in half an hour or less, the hope that we may be able to control the insanity has grown brighter with time, and is much brighter now than it was in the 1940s or '50s.

In a way, the Bomb, and the world it created, made Halfyard's death easier for me. The age in which he lived, the age in which David Hume's "Essay on Human Understanding" still mattered, ended the week he died. He could never have dreamed that I would live to see the back side of the moon, have close-up views of the satellites of Jupiter in living colour, or that, within a quarter of a century, I would be able to compute the value of pi to the one hundredth decimal place in a matter of seconds. The fastest Charlie and I had ever travelled was in a car at sixty miles an hour. A few years after his death I would be travelling through the stratosphere at the speed of sound, and others would be travelling through space at ten miles a *second*. Soon thereafter we would be entertaining doubts that Einstein's "constant" really set a limit to the powers of our technology.

Halfyard and I discussed just about everything with, it seems to me now, one notable exception. I can't recall that we ever talked about sex. Perhaps this was a deference to his frailty. How we managed to discuss Flaubert in a non-sexual context I can't now imagine. And I'm certain we talked about Oscar Wilde's life and work with none but the most cursory glance at his personal relationships and his fall from public idol to persecuted prisoner.

The opposite seemed to happen when I got together with Irving and Janet Fogwill: we'd begin with Kenneth Patchen or Karl Marx, and end with fellatio, cunnilingus and group orgies. My friendships with Halfyard and the Fogwills overlapped by about a year and a half, but I don't recall that they ever met. I don't think that they would have liked or understood each other if they had.

It is sometimes difficult for me to sort out the "influences" of that period. Was it through Fogwill that I encountered the *Books of Charles Fort*, and corresponded with that great Fortean Tiffany Thayer? (To my astonishment, Smallwood, too, had encountered Thayer many years before) It was certainly through Fogwill that I encountered the work of Raymond Souster, and then went on to meet John Sutherland, Irving Layton, Tony Frish, and other members of the *First Statement* and *Northern Review* groups. It was a time when *Direction* was published from Sydney, Nova Scotia, while Souster was still in the air force. Thirty-four years after he began having a profound effect on my education I finally met Souster in Toronto.

Throughout most of the time that I knew Halfyard, I considered myself a Christian, and a member of my father's church, into which I had been formally received by baptism. There was no way, of course, that it could continue, no way that my broadening scientific education and my reading of the philosophers could possibly be reconciled with the teachings of the Dawn Bible Students. For a while, I tried. I invented new concepts to explain such primitive beliefs as "the resurrection of the body," but, finally, no amount of rationalization would work.

Fortunately for my father and myself it wasn't a sudden "fall" into Doubt and Sin and Unbelief. He could continue to hope for a long time that I might be merely passing through one of the nights of the soul. It was a time, too, when I still considered myself a poet and could write what for me still seem to be the subtly funny lines:

> We who have only partly kept the faith
> Fall automatically into hexameters.

I must have been a series of heart-rending disappointments to poor Andrew. As a boy, I never learned to skate well (and skating, for him, was the ultimate sport). He tried to console himself when he saw me become an exceptional swimmer (he could hardly swim a stroke) but it just wasn't the same thing. Then as a teenager I refused to turn what he regarded as my great talent for music into a career—he would have dearly loved to see me become a professional musician. He refused to believe that I could be either an artist or a writer. Again, he took some consolation when he saw my first book win a national award and become a best-seller. "How I wish your grandfather could have lived to see it!" he said. But again it wasn't the same thing. Finally, as a man, I failed to develop into the Christian leader that he so confidently expected me to be.

One day after all this had happened, he told me a dream: "I dreamed that you and I were both going to the same place. It was winter, and stormy. Somehow we became separated, and I went on alone for a long time, through the wind and the snow, and I finally got there, and—do you know?—when I arrived, you were there already!"

Poor Andrew! I wish, indeed, that it had been possible for him to arrive at the detached and transcendent view of the universe that I finally did achieve, at middle age, and that I set out in my books, *Dancing on the Shore* and *The Magic Ground*.

Chapter 11

With me there was never any question of politics being more than an interlude. I had firmly settled on a writing career at least ten years before I met Smallwood; politics might be a secondary avocation, perhaps also grist for the writer's mill, but in any case was never to be more than temporary.

I had begun while still in school to fit myself quite unintentionally for the hustings. I joined the Science Club and the Current Affairs Club when I was in grade eleven, lectured to both clubs, and so gained a certain degree of self-confidence, a belief that I could stand up and present my ideas to an audience. The lectures were not papers, read from a script, but off-the-cuff presentations backed by well-prepared research. I don't remember what I discussed with the Current Affairs Club, but I recall two lectures to the Science Club—one on atomic structure, one on the unsolved problems of organic evolution. Both subjects still interest me.

Then, one day in winter after I was finished with school, I saw in the paper the notice of a debate at the Methodist College Literary Institute. My brother and I went together to hear it, and found the MCLI room adjoining Pitts Memorial Hall crowded with members and visitors. We sat at the back and enjoyed the debate, and, when it came time for it, I "spoke from the floor" for about five minutes. The little talk must have been fluent, for the members crowded around me afterwards asking who I was, and, when they found out I had been a student at Prince of Wales, inviting me to apply for membership.

I quickly discovered the ability to "turn myself on" when I got to my feet, to enter a new level of consciousness while speaking, a level where the mind worked in overdrive, coining arguments, minting images; it was a level of expression close to poetry and while you were pouring it out you had a wonderful sense of power and euphoria. I have never known anyone to describe this special state of consciousness enjoyed by the orator, but it must, I'm sure, be common to most fluent extemporaneous speakers. I soon reached the point where I could confidently stand up and lead a debate without any preparation at all, provided I had the "negative side"—which meant that the case had been opened by an opposing speaker, thus giving me arguments to refute and rebut, a takeoff point from which to fly.

Debating was only one of the institute's entertainments. The other was practising parliamentary procedure. The "business sessions," full of motions and amendments and amendments to the amendments, of laying resolutions on the table, giving notices in the correct way, and of "moving the previous question" (a form of closure) were a never-ending game of playing the meetings by the rules. Many a prominent lawyer, and a string of prime ministers, had practised their art at the MCLI.

Within a year or two I was making use of this art in the union halls, and on the radio in support of the St. John's District Labour Party. The MCLI experience also helped me to write constitutions for unions and for the Newfoundland Federation of Fishermen, and by-laws and rule books for the Writers' Union of Canada and the Periodical Writers Association of Canada. It was hardly a big step from the MCLI to politics. Indeed, Joe Smallwood and I debated, together at the MCLI, the resolution that Newfoundland should confederate with Canada, and won the debate for the affirmative before an overflow audience at the Pitts Memorial Hall long before the issue went to a public vote. Within a space of three or four years I had proven myself first as the *enfant terrible* of the labour movement, and then as the trusted disciple, and even publicly designated successor, of that political genius, Joey the Great.

The problems that stood in the way of a successful career in politics were twofold. Most important, perhaps, was the fact that I regarded writing as a far higher calling than politics. No Canadian prime minister, in my book, could compare with Stephen Leacock or E.J. Pratt. The difference was not even one of degree. I would far rather have failed as a writer than have succeeded as a politician. I was not fitted to be so much as an amateur politician. The lingering ethics of Jesus, or whoever his speech-writers were, had far too great an influence, and had been powerfully reinforced by Fabian socialism. There was no way I could regard politics as being worth pursuing unless it could become a route to real social reform.

I made three trips to Labrador in 1949, in the course of being elected and serving as the first legislative member for that immense territory (three times the size of Newfoundland). The first was on a chartered fishing boat, before the election; the second was on the Canadian National Railway ships serving that coast, as far north as Nain and Okak; the third was by mail plane to Cartwright and Red Bay in the winter, and by dog team from Red Bay to the other settlements in the Straits of Belle Isle. The experience of all that northern and primitive travel in one year was a most important part of my education, both as a man with a social conscience, and as a writer. As a boy I had never dreamed of sailing among the isles of the Caribees, or along the Spanish Main. I had dreamed, instead, of Baffin Land. Why such a remote and inhospitable place? I cannot say, but the nearly inaccessible lands of the arctic fascinated me from the days I began pouring over atlases and maps.

When at last I came to sail—in my own ship and those of my friends—I did not sail to Baffin Island, but I sailed along the coasts of Labrador, both north and south, and up to the heads of its great bays, and this came close to fulfilling my youthful dreams, for Labrador is a stark and beautiful land, forested in the south and in the deep interior, but truly arctic in climate and configuration along its coasts.

The visits I did make, eventually, to the tropics, were fascinating, but for me never compared with the eight visits I made to Labrador, and the travels I undertook there by ship, by boat, by dog team, and by bush plane. I visited not only the places everyone gets to see—Churchill Falls, Goose Bay, the mission stations in the north, but also such rarely visited places as Unknown Falls, the Torngak Mountains, and the wonderful, straight cleft of Double Mer. I saw wolves pacing along the shore of Port Manvers Run; I hunted seals in Voisey's Bay and Tasisuak Lake, saw the young ice form on Tasiuyak, and watched the northern lights dancing madly over the Okak Islands.

I believe the name of the boat I chartered from Colin Storey for my first voyage to Labrador was *Bowring Two*, but it hardly deserves to be remembered. It was a twenty-ton gasoline-driven fishing boat with the very crudest accommodation. Lee White, from Northwest River, who travelled with me as my agent and campaign manager, shared a six-by-six-foot cabin on deck with me. We slept on boards in bunks crudely knocked together. There was no toilet, so we used a bucket in the fish hold, and threw the contents over the side. We bathed in a dish pan, and ate food prepared by a man who was supposed to know how to run the engine, but who certainly didn't know how to cook. Our skipper and navigator, a former seal-killer named Rideout, was chiefly distinguished by his love for chewing tobacco and his violent language. He was the only sailor I ever knew who kept swearing at the sea. *He* wasn't afraid of the god-damned thing, he kept saying; let the god-damned ocean do its worst—he'd show it!

The *Bowring Two* was a wallower. It had no sails, just a brute of an engine that shoved it through the seas at something like seven knots. Any four-foot wave inevitably came over the bow, the side or the stern, as the case might be. Most of the time we had calm weather with sunshine, and we enjoyed the voyage, though the few puffs of wind that we did get soaked everything with salt water.

We stopped at Twillingate, Fleur de Lys, and St. Anthony, before running through Quirpon Tickle and around the northern tip of the Great Northern Peninsula to the Straits of Belle Isle and L'Anse au

Clair. After visiting the small settlements along that shore we began late the next day working our way northward past Point Amour, the narrowest part of the strait, and here we got caught in running field ice that seemed to appear from nowhere just as darkness was about to fall.

Rideout kept the boat butting and pushing against the ice pans until after dark. Then suddenly the engine raced. The propeller shaft had come uncoupled. We now drifted with the ice across a series of shallows running seaward from the north shore of the strait. By good luck we didn't hit anything. Because we were in shallow water, we dropped an anchor, and paid out anchor line to its limit. The anchor held. The line didn't. As it parted, we continued merrily on our way southward with the ice and the current.

Fortunately, Lee White knew something about engines, and had the kind of mechanical sense that native Labradormen seem to develop in infancy. He improvised a coupling, drilled holes in the shaft, and got it spliced together. By one o'clock in the morning we had power again, and were adrift somewhere in the middle of the Straits of Belle Isle. Rideout resumed his manoeuvring, this time a bit more cautiously. By four o'clock it was daylight, we were out of the ice, and heading for an anchorage between the golden sand dunes of L'Anse au Loup.

We continued the trip with one anchor, leaving the lost one on the bottom. I heard later that a local fishing crew located it and sold it to a passing ship with a crew of Labrador floaters, seasonal fishermen from Newfoundland who worked the Labrador banks from ships. The floaters we saw that summer travelled mostly in small black schooners with barked sails. Better sea boats than the Bowring Two, they sometimes passed us on their way north.

We called at just about every small settlement, and in some of them helped people fill out applications for pensions and family allowances that were three months late. Many had no documentary proof of their age. Fortunately I had been sworn in as a Justice of the Peace, so I could take affidavits and administer oaths. Thus we were able to arrange some kind of documentation for most of the applicants.

I had dealt with poor people before this, city dwellers at the bottom of the wage scale, but what I found on Labrador was poverty of a different order. Those people not only lived in the part of the province with the meagerest resources and the harshest climate, but they had to pay the highest prices because of shipping costs, and they had suffered a series of fish failures that had left many of them destitute. Here were men who had never had any employment except fishing, on a coast where there were no fish, or almost none. Unlike the floaters, they could not pack up and try their luck further north. They were stuck in the little harbours where their ancestors had jumped ship and put down roots generations ago.

In a good year a fisherman relying on the Labrador cod might earn $500. In a bad year he might earn less than $100. The women's lives orbited around the stove and the bed in houses that often had earthen floors and only two rooms. True, many of them had somewhat more substantial houses deep in the inner reaches of the bays where they could collect firewood and hunt game in winter, but it was still life on the very edge of survival, with little comfort, let alone luxury.

The men were mostly underweight, but tough and wiry. The women were haggard before they reached middle age. The children went barefoot from spring thaw to freeze-up, not always because they wished to, but because they had never owned a pair of shoes, and were lucky to have home-made sealskin boots for winter. In spite of the harshness of their lives, many of them were very beautiful. The old people sat patiently in the corners, waiting for death, it seemed to me, without pleasure or hope.

Those were my constituents. They hoisted flags and fired guns when I came to visit them. Some of them sent me Christmas cards, and even love letters. There was almost nothing I could do for them, other than seeing to it that they got the minimum social services that belonged by right to all Canadians.

The most enjoyable part of the trip was from Rigolet through the exciting tidal narrows into Lake Melville and thence, at night, through waters stained red with mingled sunset and dawn, to Northwest River. Here was life as it should be lived in the north. Like numerous others visitors in summer or winter, I fell in love with Northwest River, and indeed with the whole area at the head of Lake Melville. The people were prosperous, and loved the life they had made there for themselves. Trappers have to be ruthless toward animals, hardened to inflicting ghastly suffering on small wild creatures, but that was part of life far inland, on the trap lines. In the lovely villages where they lived they were gentle, courteous, soft-spoken. Goose Bay, of course, was a modern monster, and Happy Valley, its appended dormitory town, was in 1949 still a collection of shacks run up higgledy-piggledy during the war, and covered in fine sand and dust. I didn't foresee, at the time, that the traditional villages and their way of life would also be destroyed before the world was through with them.

Lee White and I travelled a few miles on the waters of the Lower Hamilton River, now called the Churchill, by canoe. Innu canoeists took me up Northwest River to Cape Caribou on Grand Lake. I went swimming many times in warm sea water with boys from Northwest River. I was stranded in the area for a couple of weeks because the *Bowring Two* had headed back to Newfoundland, and I couldn't get a local boat to take me to the settlements on the northern coast. Eventually Lee White and I, the election over, headed back to St. John's on the *S.S. Kyle*.

When we went on board the coastal steamer the cook took me to his galley and said: "I'll bet you'd like some civilized meat," and began slicing a huge roast of beef. I hated to admit it, but it was true. I had been eating caribou, trout, seal, pike, bear, and even porcupine for more than a month. It was all delicious. But roast beef was what I really wanted, just then. I later learned that Labrador people visiting St. John's missed wild game just as much as I missed beef and chicken and roast pork.

At Northwest River, then an idyllic village populated with some of the most charming people I had ever met, there were tensions between the settlers and the Innu, between the settlers and the Grenfell Mission, and between everyone and the Hudson Bay Company, which ran the large general store and bought most of the furs from the trappers.

The Hudson Bay Company, I found to my surprise, was disliked much less than the Grenfell Mission. People regarded the HBC as honest even if ruthless bargainers and profiteers. They regarded the Grenfell organization as foreign imperialists, living off the fat of the land, taking all the best berths for their own trout fishing, and getting large amounts of foreign aid and adulation for performing services that ought by rights to be performed by the government. The boarding school was especially unpopular among its former students. As they recalled it, life there was harsh and repressive, and filled with capricious punishments: "You'd be out weeding the mission garden, and you'd get called in for a whipping for no reason that you knew." It didn't surprise me to learn that bed-wetting was a common problem at the boarding schools—many of the children there were bitterly unhappy.

When I first visited Northwest River no people of Inuit culture lived that far south. The Inuit of the Groswater Bay area had intermarried with French and English settlers until they had disappeared. The typical "WASP" family of Northwest River was of mixed French-English-Inuit descent. Some had English names like Blake, others French or Channel Island names like Goudie and Montague, or names like White that had been "translated" into English (in this case from the widespread Acadian "LeBlanc").

Though European settlers and fur traders had intermarried freely with the Inuit, and respected the Inuit as near-equals, there had been no such cultural and familial mixing with the Innu—indeed, not much social contact at all. The Innu seemed to be proud and aloof, less eager than the Inuit to flatter the whites and to embrace every fad and gadget that the white people introduced. But in later years they, too, embraced the imported culture. By the 1960s every teen-aged Innu boy wanted to be a truck driver, and every teen-aged Innu girl wanted to live in a "real" house with a washing machine and a vacuum cleaner. Many of them achieved their ambitions, along with vast doses of unhappiness.

In 1949 the Innu lived by themselves in tents on the right bank of the river, where only two or three small houses belonged to settlers. Everyone else lived on the left bank, where the Grenfell Mission had its living quarters, its hospital, its school, its greenhouses and workshops, and its corps of "wops" (foreign volunteers WithOut Pay), mostly young Americans from wealthy families doing their bit for the lesser breeds while getting a taste of the wild north strong and free. There, too, the Hudson Bay Company had its store, and the government had its Ranger Force detachment. Except among the Innu, the Rangers had little to do at Northwest River, where people were educated, industrious, self-reliant, and law-abiding, but in the tiny coves scattered around the outer reaches of the bay there were cases of destitution as bad as those I had met along the barren outer shore, even a few people who had been partially disabled for life by extreme poverty and malnutrition in early childhood. The children of the Northwest River settlers had no such problems; almost without exception they were healthy, bright, fine-looking kids, filled with enthusiasm for life. I wish fervently that they could have grown up to be independent and self-reliant people of the wilderness like their fathers and mothers. What actually happened to most of them was that they wound up working for wages at Goose Bay, Labrador City, or Wabush, acquiring colour TV sets and VCRs, cars, boats, ATVs and skidoos, and in rare cases even private airplanes, but losing their independence and their joy of life.

There was one girl in particular whose beauty moved me very deeply. She was barely past childhood—sixteen to eighteen perhaps?—and with a child's mingled shyness and eagerness to please. She was the first girl I met whom I might, given the right circumstances, have married. I inquired about her once or twice in later years. She wedded a local man, of course, and they moved to Happy Valley, where he worked. Ten years after I first met her she was already sinking into a faded, grossly overweight middle age, her teenage beauty only a memory. To my mind, the boys who drowned themselves in boating accidents on the Hamilton River suffered a less tragic fate.

There was considerable tension between whites and Innu—mainly a question of trapping grounds. The white trappers travelled far inland, to places such as Unknown River, Grand Falls (now Churchill Falls) and the great lake named Michikamau, parcelling out the country between them so that they did not encroach on one another's trap lines. The Innu had never been part of this system. They travelled in small bands and families, living off the land, trapping where they could, often on traditional hunting grounds that were now claimed as trap lines by the settlers. White people who were otherwise tolerant, and who certainly would not have regarded the Inuit as a "problem" had they lived further north, spoke often about the "Indian problem," and pondered how it could be settled. So far as I could see, there was no way to settle it, short of the Innu giving up their traditional migratory lives and becoming poor whites like the Inuit.

I made my third trip by mail plane and dog team that winter, flying to Cartwright and Red Bay and several places between with a wonderful bush pilot named Eric Blackwood, who had been a Royal Air Force captain in the Second World War, and had subsequently founded Eastern Provincial Airways. I had flown with him previously in a Norseman. We now flew in a new Beaver, as yellow as a buttercup and as agile as a deer. Eric was totally in love with the thing. "What an airplane!" he used to chortle. To demonstrate its abilities at Frenchman's Island he took off from the ice of the harbour straight toward the side of a hill, then zoomed over the crest and circled around a cloud.

Having just turned twenty-six, I was too young at the time to be bothered by derring-do. It was exactly the kind of thing I might have done myself. Eric flew mainly by landmarks. At one point we zigzagged back and forth along the coast looking for a large shed with a red roof, which was supposed to guide us into a settlement. At another, when we were caught in an unexpected snowstorm, we descended to less than a hundred feet, and banked back and forth over the ice floes.

"What the hell are you doing?" I shouted over the noise in the cockpit.

"Looking for a nice smooth place to land," he shouted back, "a place we can take off from when the snow stops."

We were untold miles from anywhere. Fortunately, the ice was rough, and the ice pans too small for a safe takeoff, even in a Beaver, so Eric was forced to look for a harbour, which he fortunately found before dark, and we landed and spent the night in a house instead of in an unheated airplane.

On the return trip we called at St. Anthony, and there made the only perpendicular landing I have ever experienced in a fixed-wing aircraft. The surface wind was blowing at about fifty miles an hour, which matched, approximately, the Beaver's landing speed with lowered flaps. Eric pointed the plane into the wind, and we settled toward the ice, tilting a little from side to side, with no forward speed whatever. As the skis touched, he quickly raised the flaps, but not quite quickly enough. We took off to a height of five or six feet, flew sideways for a short distance, then landed again with a jolt.

"Nice work, that!" he commented, and gunned the engine to taxi to the wharf, where a small crowd had gathered to watch the performance and welcome us ashore.

I hope I haven't made Blackwood sound like a reckless pilot. He was a great flyer, and took no chances that he didn't consider necessary. At least once he landed with skis on the sandy shore of an unfrozen lake. Once he pancaked onto the ice when an engine failed on takeoff, and created a spider web of cracks without plunging through. He had a few minor accidents, and as he approached middle age he decided to give up flying because, as he explained to me, he'd been pushing his luck, and sooner or later it would run out. Perhaps the most dangerous and freakish accident of all happened in the winter on Labrador when he took off from an unfamiliar harbour on skis, unaware that an unmarked telegraph wire stretched across the ice from side to side. The skis hooked the wire, the wire held, and the plane turned turtle, landing on the ice on its back, facing in the opposite direction. A tank, installed behind the cockpit, tore loose, and smashed the instrument panel inches from Blackwood's head. He was uninjured, but had escaped death by a handspan.

To prepare for the winter trip to Labrador I'd bought my first heavy parka, with padding, and a hood surrounded by wolverine fur, heavy woollen work socks, and lined overshoes. I tried wearing sealskin boots like the natives, but found them much less satisfactory than lined rubber boots made in the south, with slippers worn inside. In this unorthodox dress my feet were never cold, as those of my dog driver, who wore sealskin boots, nearly always were.

The heavy clothing, as it turned out, was a good idea, because the temperatures along the Labrador Coast that winter, even in the Straits of Belle Isle, hovered around thirty below zero Fahrenheit, which wouldn't be too bad on a windless day in the centre of a continent, but was murderously cold on a coastline with open water never more than a few miles offshore, and wind blowing at twenty or thirty miles an hour.

I have forgotten the name of the man who agreed to take me with his dog team from Red Bay to L'Anse au Clair and back to Forteau, but he was reputed to have the best team in the area, to be a winter traveller of great experience, and indeed was the only man who would do it, because there was no snow on the high ground, and consequently no trail that you could travel in any comfort.

We travelled along chains of lakes whenever possible, riding on the komatik, while the dogs slipped and slid and scrabbled for a foothold. When we had to cross bare ground the dogs could not haul us, so we had to chase the sled at a brisk trot, the speed at which the dogs themselves moved. We trailed a long rope behind the sled, so we could grab it and prevent the team from getting away if we tripped and fell, or had to stop for any other reason. Running behind the sled in all that heavy clothing wasn't easy work. In the course of a week I lost nine pounds, and we both suffered a bit from frostbite on the small areas of our faces that were exposed to the wind.

After the first day a stray dog began following our sled. He seemed to be half starved, but wouldn't come when called. However, when we stopped in a settlement that night he joined the other dogs to be fed, and was caught, tied, and added to the team,

The one dangerous thing that we did was near Cape Diable, where the trail ran along a ledge above a cliff. The ledge sloped outward toward the edge of the cliff, and was covered with ice. We rounded this incredibly dangerous spot with the driver shouting at the dogs to keep moving, the dogs, well aware of the peril, scrabbling at the ice with every claw, and the sled, with both of us aboard, veering sideways toward the edge and the ice-covered rocks below. I've been in car wrecks and planes with engine failure, and at sea in hurricane-force winds, but I still regard that sled ride as my most hair-raising experience.

The hardest labour was crossing The Battery, a cliff-like hill that runs out to the headland near Forteau. There was no way the dogs could climb to the top. We had to unhitch the komatik, clamber up the ice-covered ledges ourselves, and haul the komatik with its load up by hand, using the long rope, hitched around a rock like a windlass. Once we had the sled on top, we had to haul up the dogs, yelping and protesting and in fear of their lives as they involuntarily ascended the ice fall. Then we tackled them in again, rode over the top, and went sliding down the other side at a crazy rate, with a piece of chain hung over the front runners to act as a brake (a "drug" the driver called it) while the dogs fled downhill for their lives with the komatik bouncing crazily behind.

From L'Anse au Clair we returned to L'Anse au Loup, and then to Forteau. Snow had arrived, and made the going much easier. At Forteau I paid off the driver with warm thanks. I could well understand why no other dog driver would agree to make the trip, but from now on he would have a decent trail for whatever travelling he did for the rest of the winter.

I slept, during that trip, in one house so badly built that snow actually sifted through the seams and collected on the bed where I was sleeping. I don't know how the family managed, but they probably gave me the best bed in the house, as they would naturally do for any visitor from the outside.

For me, the greatest hardship that winter was making do without either inside toilets or outside privies. The only place I could find even the most primitive privy was at L'Anse au Loup, where there was an old double privy next to the school. Everywhere else, you either used a hole through the floor of a fish shed above the landwash, or a bucket that you also emptied into the sea. While travelling, it wasn't so bad. You just did your job behind the nearest rock, in the greatest haste to avoid freezing. When I got back to Forteau, where Blackwood planned to pick me up on his next trip, the nurse invited me to stay at the little cottage hospital, and I must admit that I was thoroughly grateful for the indoor comforts of civilization for a change.

It was a time when you still paid for hospital services, no matter how poor you were, and some of the people paid their bills by bringing in game from the surrounding barrens. We dined on varying hares and a bit of caribou. In fact, the hunting had been rather good, and one man took me to his storehouse to show me more than a hundred grouse, along with some seabirds, hung by their feet in neat lines. At another house a woman whose husband was dead proudly showed me the birds and game she'd hunted herself. The men grudgingly admitted to me that she was one of the best shots in the village.

Someone had paid his hospital bill, at least in part, by presenting the nurse with the carcass of a snowy owl, which we had, one day, for dinner, stuffed and roasted exactly like a goose, though it had a distressingly human-like shape when plucked and roasted. The meat smelled most appetizing, and looked delicious on the centre of the table, crackling brown, but had much the same consistency as a motor car tire. Perhaps it was the great-great-grandfather of the owls that had come south from the tundra that winter.

The nurse had sole charge of the little hospital, doing her best to act as doctor and nurse. Sometimes she wasn't equal to the task, or perhaps her patients were beyond medical aid. While I was there she lost a small baby whose mother had brought it to the hospital with pneumonia too late to save its life. The nurse sat up with the baby all night, trying to keep its breath from failing, but the child died before dawn. It was the only time I ever saw a nurse break down and weep.

In those trips to Labrador (and later, in spring and autumn as well as summer), I gained some insight into the lives of people living in very primitive conditions on the edge of survival. But the most socially useful thing that came out of it was the realization, gained on my winter trip, that it was possible to build a highroad along the Labrador side of the Straits of Belle Isle connecting the settlements between L'Anse au Clair and Red Bay, thus serving a quarter of Labrador's permanent population with a road. I started the process immediately by organizing roads boards in every settlement, and having them apply to the government for grants. They would build roads and bridges at half pay in their own settlements, and towards neighbouring settlements. Once a road of some kind existed, the Roads Division of the Department of Public Works could be expected to improve it and make it permanent.

By this means the first highroad in Labrador came into existence. I submitted a plan with a map (of which I still have a copy) to the Department. It arranged tiny grants to local roads boards. Within a few years the highroad actually existed, and eventually a ferry linked it to roads in Newfoundland.

That was one of the two useful things I did as member for Labrador. The other was the organization of the Division of Northern Labrador Services in the Department of Welfare to replace the Northern Labrador Trading Operation, which was run by the Department of Resources, and had taken over the northern posts of the Hudson Bay Company. The great advantage of the Division of Northern Labrador

Services, which continued to run the trading posts as one of its activities, was that it became responsible for the welfare of the people in every way: it was to assure not only trade goods at reasonable prices, but assistance to fisheries, public housing, education, health and welfare. Over the course of the next twenty years the Division gradually transformed the living conditions of the people of northern Labrador from that of stone-age tribesmen to that of twentieth-century Canadians. To do so the Division drew upon the resources of both provincial and federal governments.

For the second time in my life (the first was in the labour movement) I felt I had justified my existence, and could die tomorrow, knowing that I had done something well worthwhile.

Chapter 12

The spring following my winter trip to Labrador I bought my own ship, a 45-foot sloop-rigged yacht, the *Fort Amadjuak*, from Ralph Parsons, recently retired chief fur commissioner of the Hudson Bay Company. I paid $3,000 cash for her, and because I had no money, Attorney General Les Curtis backed a note for me at his branch of the Bank of Nova Scotia in St. John's. I then transferred my own account from the Canadian Bank of Commerce to the Bank of Nova Scotia, and have continued to deal with that bank ever since. I paid off the note out of my sessional indemnities and travelling allowances. By good luck, we had an extra session that year, and I was out of debt within twelve months.

The *Fort Amadjuak* was a beautiful little ship built by the Villion Frères fur trading company for its Labrador operations, and sold to the HBC when that company bought out the Villion Frères posts. She was built at Shelburne, Nova Scotia, with white oak timbers and pitch pine planking throughout—inside as well as outside her ribs, making her very strong for her size. She was sheathed in greenheart, for safe navigation in ice. Fitted comfortably like a yacht, her cabin was easily converted from a bedroom to a chart room and dining room. Her fo'castle was designed to sleep a crew of two, or even four at a pinch. There were brass fittings on deck, brass rails on the companionway, brass risers on the steps, and brass hardware in the cabin. She had a sixteen-horsepower Gardner diesel auxiliary engine, which could push her along at about seven knots, but under sail she could do better than that. I averaged nine and a quarter knots throughout one memorable sailing day when conditions were perfect, with a quartering wind and a favourable tide between Rigolet and Cartwright.

I hired a retired mariner, a grand old man in his seventies, who had been a first mate in the government coastal service, to accompany me to Labrador in 1950. He knew his way into and out of the major Labrador harbours where the coastal ships made their calls. I had learned the way into and out of some of the others the summer before. Between us, we could go just about anywhere, though neither of us had any experience in handling a ship under sail.

We got our experience the first day out of Bay Roberts, where I'd bought the ship and had her overhauled. The engine failed, and we tried to tack back into harbour against the wind. We could tack, alright, but could make no forward progress. Eventually, a fisherman in a trap boat took pity on us and towed us in to the wharf. An ignominious start, indeed. But we found the trouble with the engine, a mere matter of air locks in the fuel injectors, and set out again next day.

Going into Bonavista, after a first stop at Carbonear, I insisted on taking the run inside the island, where the chart showed plenty of water, instead of the outside ship's run, which the old skipper had always used. This took us close to the land, and collected an admiring crowd of fishermen at the wharf.

"My! What a grand little craft!" one of them said as we tied up. "She looked all alive in the water as she came along there."

I could feel my heart swell with pride. I felt that way about her myself. I'd stand back and look at her on moorings, and say to myself, "God! It can't really be true that she's mine." I came perhaps as close to loving the *Fort Amadjuak* as you can come to loving any inanimate thing. I well understood the feeling among some yachtsmen and professional sailors that ships have souls.

We travelled through the lovely inside waters of Dildo Run, visited Twillingate and St. Anthony, and, of course, all sorts of places along the coast of Labrador. We even ran inland to Port Hope Simpson along one of the landlocked waterways, and into the inner end of

Sandwich Bay, to Separation Point, where the little ship lay far over on her side on a sand bank when the tide fell to dead low.

Labrador that summer was a delight. But we weathered one terrible storm between Cartwright and Rigolet, where there is a long stretch of harbourless coast. The skipper stayed at the wheel, with the little ship all but hove to much of the time, fighting the sea with amazing strength for a man of his advanced years. When he looked like his strength might fail, I went below and fetched him a drink of gin.

"That saved my life," he gasped above the uproar. "Perhaps we can anchor under Saddle Island, if we can get that far." He was shouting into my ear.

At Saddle Island the wind seemed to be dropping.

"If you can handle her for half an hour, I think we can run on for Rigolet," he said. "The wind will be on the quarter and we'll have some shelter from the north side of the bay."

He watched me taking the waves on the port bow for five minutes while the lee rail dipped under, then staggered below for a brief rest. The bay narrowed, the sea became calmer despite the howling wind. As soon as we could see signs of land ahead, we altered course and ran in to Rigolet in triumph.

"You didn't actually run through that storm!" the HBC post manager exclaimed as we tied up.

"How do you think we got here?" I laughed.

"I was on the radio to St. Mary's Harbour," he said. "They reported the wind there at a hundred miles an hour on their wind gauge."

"I don't think it got above eighty where we were," the old skipper growled.

"What a wonderful little ship you have!" the manager exclaimed. "I wish I owned her."

"You're not the first who's told me that," I said. "The Grenfell doctors would like to have her, too."

That day was an exception. Usually the weather was warm and sunny, and the winds light. I spent most of my time on deck barefoot, wearing only a pair of jeans, but running into harbour I'd say regretfully, "I'll have to put on a shirt, I suppose." "Yes," the skipper would agree. "Otherwise your constituents will say, 'I knew him when he didn't have a shirt to his name.'"

We had a few minor misadventures. Running under power into one harbour where a big freighter was moored, I was towing a line of laundry in the prop wash to clean it, when I suddenly realized that we were in danger of being dismasted by an overhead steel cable stretching from the ship to the shore. I slammed the little engine into reverse, and put it full speed astern—just in time. The masthead did, indeed, touch the cable, but too lightly to do any damage. That wasn't the end of our problem. The laundry, and the rope to which it was attached, had wrapped themselves firmly around the propeller and the shaft, and no amount of probing with a boat hook from the dingy would dislodge the mess. I tried lashing a chisel to the boat hook, but that did no good, either. In the end I had to dive into the ice-cold water with a knife, and hack the stuff loose. It took three dives, and chilled me to the marrow, but saved us from having to beach the ship.

On the passage from Northwest River to Goose Bay we again ran into trouble. You have to stay far offshore to avoid sandbanks, and everything in the immediate vicinity is so low-lying that there are no effective landmarks from which to triangulate yourself on a chart. I was relying on a series of buoys set out to guide ships into Goose Bay from the open sea, and was using the spy glass that my grandfather had used on his foreign voyages half a century before. But I missed the outermost buoy, mistook the one next inshore for it, and ran the little ship hard aground.

We tried backing off with the engine, but she wouldn't budge. We tried alternate fore and aft surges in the hope of gradually digging a channel in the sand. The tide was very nearly full, so there'd be no help from that source. Finally we took the anchor out as far as it would go in the dingy, fastened it to the mast near the cross-trees, and, with the aid of a pulley, took enough strain on the anchor line to tip the ship over so that her keel came up out of the sand, and we were thus able to drag her on her side into slightly deeper water. We then recovered the anchor, and inched our way seaward, dead slow, until we picked up the outermost buoy, and finally arrived in Goose Bay about three hours late.

There seemed to be no damage from the grounding, so we continued our voyage. It was impossible to buy diesel fuel anywhere in Labrador that year, so I bought a drum of stove oil at Hopedale, and used it sparingly, relying on the sails alone whenever possible for the homeward voyage. The engine didn't really enjoy running on stove oil. It coughed and complained but kept going whenever it was needed.

When we put the *Fort Amadjuak* on dock at St. Anthony, we discovered that we had put a slight bend in one of the bronze blades of the propeller during our efforts to get her out of the sand. Otherwise there had been no damage in the grounding off Goose Bay.

On that trip we made only one night run, from St. Anthony direct to Twillingate, the old skipper at the wheel, and I in the forepeak, staring into the murky darkness, worrying myself half sick over nothing. We were on course, with no land near, and surely anything at sea would have a light showing! Nevertheless, it was with a great sense of relief that I finally picked up the lighthouse on Twillingate Island—dead ahead, just as it should be. I realized right then that I didn't have the makings of a master mariner any more than those of a successful politician because I simply couldn't delegate authority in matters of life and death—I could never have gone asleep, leaving the ship in charge of a junior officer. Captain John, in fact, had much the same failing. He cat-napped on his voyages, of course, but often paced his deck for days and nights at a stretch, and never went below for more than a few minutes at a time if he believed real seamanship was needed.

From Twillingate south we again had perfect weather, and crossing the mouth of Bonavista Bay we broke out our last two cold beers, kept at sea temperature in a tiny outside locker, to celebrate. But after we rounded Cape Baccalieu into Conception Bay we had almost a dead calm, and had to use our last few gallons of stove oil to reach Holyrood, where I had decided to tie up for the night. We arrived in late afternoon in glass calm, and then motored to St. John's. All our batteries were dead, so we had no working radio on the ship at that point, and only on reaching the city by car did I hear that a hurricane was supposed to be heading for Newfoundland. By that time it was dark, and I was dead tired. Too late, I decided, to do anything about the *Fort Amadjuak*, moored to the public wharf at Holyrood, with all of Conception Bay, not to mention the North Atlantic, open behind her. Anyway, it didn't look much like hurricane weather to me. There was hardly a puff of wind, and I guessed that the hurricane was veering out toward mid-ocean along the southern slope of the Grand Bank. I collapsed into bed and slept an exhausted sleep, leaving my little ship in the lap of God.

Next morning the sun was shining, and there was a ten-knot breeze from the west. The hurricane was somewhere east of the banks, "blowing itself out in mid-Atlantic" as they used to say. Perhaps if Captain John had been alive he might have repeated one of the remarks he used to make when he heard of people getting by on luck instead of good judgment: "I always said that God looked after fools."

Chapter 13

I sailed the *Fort Amadjuak* on short runs in Conception Bay that autumn, and often lived aboard on weekends. I swam by diving from her deck, cooked in her galley, slept in her cabin, worked at the chart table. Finally I drained off the water and left her on her moorings for the winter. She seemed quite secure and dry. I visited her occasionally to try the hand pump, but she was still a sound boat: there was never any water in the bilge.

In the spring I discovered that the engine had made its last voyage. There was a small leak in the water-jacket. When I tried to patch it, matters just got worse. The entire water-jacket was so corroded that it would have to be condemned—virtually the same thing as saying that the engine was finished.

Not only that, the sails were in bad shape. They could serve as spares, but the mainsail, at least, would have to be replaced before another lengthy voyage. New sails could be sewn at St. John's, where one small sail loft was still struggling to survive, but the mainsail would cost about a thousand dollars. I might be able to buy a used engine for another thousand. Then I would have to put her on dock and pay for installation. At the absolute minimum, it looked like about three thousand dollars. She'd need some new rigging, too, and a bank of storage batteries to replace those that had gone dead. (I had run with oil lamps on the southward voyage the previous summer). By the time I had done all the shopping and estimating, it was obvious that I would not be able to make a voyage to Labrador that year.

I was in a quandary: keep the ship and go into debt for two years at least? Sell her and try to canvass Labrador by public transport? I decided to sell for what I could get, and quickly found a buyer, a small fish firm in Bay Roberts willing to pay $1500. Andrews Labrador Fisheries took her to convert her into a work boat. It was a sad day when I bade my small ship goodbye, but there seemed to be little choice,

Don Andrews, who had inherited Andrews Labrador Fisheries from his father, did a lot to introduce me to fish buyers, fish packers, owners of small fish plants—the sort of people among whom he moved. He assumed I was going to remain Member for Labrador, and a close friend of Smallwood. Hence, I was someone worth cultivating. More than that, we enjoyed each other's company, and became fast friends. His firm had a premises at Frenchman's Island, Labrador, and one of the first artificial fish dryers in Newfoundland, at Bay Roberts. The dryers were still experimental: they scarcely paid their way. But within a few years they were putting sun-cured fish out of business, and bringing an end to the ancient outport waterfront with its tiers of fish flakes. The dryers did best with heavily salted fish, so were welcomed by people dealing in the Labrador cure. Unfortunately, they could not reproduce anything resembling shore cure, and this superior kind of salt fish almost vanished from the world—a great pity, since it was the only kind of salt cod really worth eating. In subsequent years Bill Morry of Ferryland made great efforts to save shore cure, and I suspect the time will come when we'll be able to buy it again, at a premium price, just as you can buy good bread, made by private bakers from whole grains, and just as you can buy organically grown apples, if you are willing to look far enough and pay enough for them.

Don and I knocked around Conception Bay together, made one or two motor trips as far as Bonavista, drank a lot of rum, and talked about fisheries development. Unfortunately, there was nothing I could do to help the fishing industry. For the first few years after Confederation it staggered forward from one crisis to the next, and seemed to be dying on its feet. It didn't begin to recover until unemployment insurance was extended to fishermen in 1957, after which this basic industry made a dramatic recovery, not only in Newfoundland, but in Nova Scotia, and to a lesser extent in the other Atlantic Provinces.

I got to know a lot of fishermen and a lot of fishing masters in those years. Some of them were men who had devoted their lives to the fishery, and had invested a lot of money and effort in it. They earned my deep respect, and I became very angry when I saw the fishery so grossly misunderstood, misinterpreted and mismanaged by "experts" in Ottawa and Mainlanders at St. John's.

Among the worst misinterpretations was the one made famous (among Mainlanders) by a Mainland economist named Parzival Copes, who worked for a while at Memorial University in Newfoundland. Copes, sitting in his chair at Memorial, developed a "theory" of the fishery as a "haven for the unemployed" and as the "employer of last resort" in the Atlantic Provinces, the industry to which people turned when they had failed at everything else. Had Copes mixed freely with fishermen, as I did for many years, first as a politician, and then as a journalist (I even helped to haul a few cod traps myself), he could never have made such an error. The fishery, among outport Newfoundlanders, is the employer of first choice, not last, and it is one Canada's basic productive industries, like wheat farming.

People choose to work at the fishery for a number of reasons so long as it will give them a living. Most important, perhaps, it is self-employment, and no one who has ever been successfully self-employed would exchange it for a nine-to-five job at three times the money. This is a fact that Joe Smallwood, with his chant of "good cash wages," never understood. Also important; it produced a real product, a valuable article of real wealth that you can see and handle and even eat. How different that is from helping some multi-national corporation poison the environment! How different from making disposable diapers! How different from drawing graphs on a desk in a university! Also important: you get to do most of your work outdoors, in a boat or a ship or on the waterfront, using your back and limbs in a healthy way. How different from pushing buttons or totting up figures on a computer, or doing any of those other meaningless tasks that any weakling could perform just as well! Also important: the fishery uses skills that you learned as a child, from older members of your family or clan; it calls upon accumulated experience, the fruit of centuries. And, perhaps not least important: the fishery is a whole-life experience: you must learn to operate and maintain and repair engines; you must learn to use woodworking tools with skill and precision, and to maintain and repair them; you must learn to knit twine; you must learn elementary seamanship; and you learn that the time you spend working for yourself, building your own house, keeping it in repair, cultivating your own garden, producing your own fuel, gives you far greater return in terms of real wealth—the value of the product to you and your family—than the same time spent producing something for sale. Only an ignorant Mainland economist could ever have regarded a fisherman as unemployed, or semi-employed, or under-employed, while according the accolade of full employment to those producing scented arse-wipes for babies or plastic toys for cats.

Unemployment insurance, and other forms of subsidy, saved the fishery, at least for one generation, and so saved one of the basic industries that keep Canada alive. Such subsidies are no more than elementary justice. It is entirely proper and just that people who spend their lives producing trash or poisons or fake foods should be taxed to help support the production of real wealth, whether it be timber or wheat or fish or houses or clothing or fuel, and whether it be produced for the market or for the family.

I had little more than two years to devote my attention to such basic problems as the future of the fishery in Newfoundland. By the summer of 1950, Dr. Alfred Valdmanis had arrived in St. John's to direct Smallwood's vision of economic development, and Joe Smallwood was no longer approachable by his former associates on any major issue. The era of the Smallwood-Valdmanis government had begun, and it was time for the rest of us to begin looking for something besides politics to occupy our minds.

When I began lobbying for a Division of Northern Labrador Services to replace the Northern Labrador Trading Operation, and insisted that its proper place was in the Department of Welfare, I had the enthusiastic support of the Minister of Welfare, Dr. H.L. Pottle. It was he who got the proposal accepted by the cabinet. I put my own name into competition for director of the division, and would certainly have been accepted by the government committee making the appointment (I was still one of Smallwood's white-haired boys at that point) but I withdrew as soon as I learned that Walter Rockwood was interested in the appointment.

In my opinion he was better qualified than I. He had extensive experience on Labrador as a member of the Newfoundland Ranger Force, was universally liked and respected by the Labrador people, and had ideas concerning their needs that entirely coincided with my own. His division set about doing exactly as I had intended it to do, promoting public housing, public schools (to replace the mission schools), public water supplies, and such innovations as small community electric systems and community freezers to handle fish and game. Moreover, the post managers were now regular government servants, not expected to earn their keep out of the trading operation. The posts were expected to sell their trade goods at or near their landed cost.

Roy Hammond, who was posted to Davis Inlet, had been a partner of the trader Dick White back in the days before the Second World War, had then served in the war and lost the sight of an eye, but nevertheless returned to Nain in 1950. He shared the outlooks and beliefs that motivated the organization of the Division of Northern Labrador Services. Davis Inlet was an especially sensitive post because it was the trading centre for the northern band of the Innu, a people much more vulnerable than the Inuit, who had adapted more readily to the incursion of settlers and traders.

Roy met his wife, Anna Curran, at St. John's through me. She was an experienced teacher, and after she went with him to Labrador she became the first teacher in the Indian school at Davis Inlet. Later, she was principal of the federally financed Indian school at Northwest River, where she did a great deal to help Innu students of high school age make the transition from the migratory hunting life of their ancestors to the life on the outskirts of civilization to which the march of events had condemned them. I visited the Hammonds in Labrador a number of times, at Nain, at Davis Inlet, and at Northwest River. Through Roy Hammond I also met the legendary trader Dick White, and the lively Inuit women of his family. He became the original for my archetypal wise man, Ricardo, in the Labrador novel, *White Eskimo*, I wrote twenty years later. I firmly believe that the trends Rockwood and I and people like the Hammonds initiated did a great deal to ease the suffering that was inevitable when stone-age cultures were thrust willy-nilly into the twentieth century.

My decision not to stand for re-election on November 26, 1951 took Joe Smallwood completely by surprise. Some months earlier Ted Russell, then Minister of Mines and Resources, and I had confided our discontents to each other, our disappointment with the way the government and the party were moving, our conviction that the economic development scheme run by Smallwood and Valdmanis was heading for disaster. Soon after that Russell had resigned, and joined the CCF Party. I had no wish to make political waves. I just decided that for me the game was over, and said so to one or two other members of the House—perhaps to Phil Forsey, a close friend of mine, and Gordon Janes. Joe heard about it, and invited me for a drive in his car. We drove around the outskirts of St. John's and part way around Conception Bay while he tried to probe the basis of my discontent, and did his best to change my mind.

"First of all," he said, "you should realize that you have a *great* political future. You've heard me say in the House that you'd be premier one day. I meant it. You're the only man in the party both young enough and able enough to succeed me as party leader. But I suppose you're in a hurry. Young men are always in a hurry. I was in a hurry myself back in Squires's time. I'll make a deal with you. Hold on to your seat, and I'll give you a cabinet post at the first opportunity, the first opening. You'll be the next person appointed to the cabinet."

"But Joe, you see, that isn't what I want. I don't *want* a career in politics. I want to be a writer."

"Well... you can be a writer and a politician too. You'll have lots of time to write."

"That's not the way I see it."

"Well... what else can I offer you? Politics is the greatest career there is, the greatest way you can serve the people, your country...."

I can't remember it all, of course. We talked for at least an hour. There was no ill-feeling between us, and when Joe made his announcement to the House he was generous, flattering, describing me as an artist who wanted to devote himself to such pursuits as music and writing, and saying what a loss it was that I would not be continuing in public life. So the first of Smallwood's "heirs apparent" faded from the political scene. His choice as my successor in Labrador, and eventually as his own successor as Premier, was a man of the most conservative, unimaginative temperament, former school principal and former Deputy Minister of Welfare F.W. Rowe, who became Minister of Mines and Resources in 1952.

Where was I to go next? At the moment, nowhere. I was devoting myself to the organization of the Division of Northern Labrador Services. It took my full time, and like most of the other important things I had done in my life—the early union organizing, the creation of *Protocol*, the battle for Confederation—it was done without pay.

But the time came, early in 1952, when I had to think about how I was going to pursue my career as a writer and earn a living. By that time I had published a few poems in little magazines—*Northern Review*, *Inferno*, *Contemporary Verse*, *Protocol*, perhaps in *Suck Egg Mule* and other fringe journals of the American *avant garde*. I had published critical and other essays in *Protocol*, *Northern Review*, *Dalhousie Review*, and *Saturday Night*. Perhaps a promising beginning for a career as one of the *literati*, so long as you didn't have to earn a living from it. People who wrote that kind of thing all had jobs as editors, or more often, as university professors.

My biggest problem, though, was not the paltry nature of the earnings from such work, but my own restlessness and lack of discipline. Even when I had commissions to fulfil, as I did from *Northern Review* and *Saturday Night*, I invariably put off doing anything about them until a day or two before the deadline. The discipline of sitting down to regular hours at a typewriter seemed to be beyond me. There was always something more interesting to do, whether it was composing a poem while walking in the country, or writing parts for two flutes in an orchestral passage that would never see the light of day, although I believe such passages may still exist, somewhere among my discarded papers.

I thought about my work habits for a while, and finally said to myself: "There's only one way you are ever going to learn to *work* at writing, instead of playing at it. You've got to get a job on a newspaper, where you'll have to sit at the typewriter every day of the week and meet deadlines. After two years of that, you'll be able to work on your own."

I had been back and forth to Montreal a number of times, and was friendly with John Sutherland, the editor of *Northern Review*. I was sure he'd recommend me for a job in the city, which, more than Toronto, was then the literary capital of Canada. Perhaps the editor of *Saturday Night* would also recommend me. But my best recommendation would be a series of feature articles on Labrador that I had written and published in *The Evening Telegram* in 1950. They were full-length, fully professional, looked like the work of a real journalist, and would be the showpiece in any portfolio I presented when looking for a job.

My long-term aim was to work for about two years as a staff writer, then go freelance, and finally move on from writing for magazines and newspapers to writing and publishing books. I still had no clear idea as to what kind of books I wanted to write. Fiction was at the back of my mind, because the novel was still regarded as the central literary art form in the English language—"the thing that every writer would do if he could." I made a number of clumsy, half-hearted attempts to start writing novels in those years. I discovered some of my deficiencies, though. I discovered that I couldn't write dialogue worth a damn, and had only a very juvenile idea of how a plot was developed. Those were things I was going to have to learn. I had other deficiencies that I didn't discover until much later, among them the inability to give a story *presence*, drama, to make it happen, rather than telling about it. I would have tried something like *Prester John* or *Greenmantle* if I'd had the ability. I completed one full-length adventure story of about 60,000 words, and even submitted it to a publisher before destroying it and putting fiction aside for ten years.

I continued to think of Montreal as the place to be if you were interested in a serious literary career, or even a serious career in journalism. But my father, on hearing me discuss the matter, suggested that I should start in St. John's.

"If you succeed here you'll have a much better chance in Montreal," he argued, and though I didn't really trust his judgment (he still thought I'd thrown away a career as a musician), it sounded reasonable. So I went to see Jim Herder, the general manager of *The Evening Telegram*, who had bought my articles on Labrador.

"We could certainly do with someone to report the new session of the House of Assembly," he told me, "and since you can write, and you know how the House works, and most of the people who'll be in it, I'd be willing to give you a try."

I was paid by the session—$15 for each sitting of the House, $30 if there was as session in the evening as well as the afternoon. Rarely, there might be only four sittings a week, usually at least five, and, when Joey got impatient, the House might sit four nights a week. So I could expect to earn $75 most weeks, and a whopping $135 some weeks late in the session. This seems like nothing, nowadays, but wasn't bad pay in 1952, when you had to be pretty damn good at whatever you were doing to earn as much as $100 a week. You could finance a new house, or a new car, just about any year on such an income. My seven fat years had begun. Or, if you like, my temptation in the wilderness. It wouldn't be long before I began to *enjoy* affluence.

I was still friendly with Smallwood. He was interested in the kind of reporting I was doing, a new style for the Newfoundland legislature. He offered suggestions on how I could make the House seem livelier to the public. Report things from the visitors' galleries, he suggested; talk to the staff about their work. He did think I was a bit too generous with the space I assigned to the opposition. "But I suppose that's natural," he admitted. "You have to make them look at least *presentable*, and they certainly need all the help they can get."

I was proud of my work as a legislative reporter. I'd set a new pace, established new standards, had the reporters of the press gallery struggling to keep up with me. It was too easy a victory. The real struggle was yet to come, when the fight would not be with other journalists, but with the government itself.

Chapter 14

When I walked into Jim Herder's office to ask for a job in 1952, we already knew each other fairly well. I'd first met him back in 1947 when *The Telegram's* newsboys were on strike, and I was organizer for the Newfoundland Federation of Labour. Jim was a quiet, kindly, heavy-set man in early middle age, from a family that in youth were fine athletes, but tended to die prematurely of heart attacks—"long before their time" as Newfoundlanders of his generation would have said.

The newsboys, aged about ten to thirteen, had gotten together and demanded an increase in their commissions. They were getting one cent for each paper they sold, They went on strike for twenty cents a dozen, and put on such a good show with picket lines, placards, and daily front-page coverage from *The Telegram's* rival, *The Daily News*, that the Federation authorized me to intervene. By then I had reached the peak of my career in labour, and was chairman both of the General Workers Union and the Building Trades Council.

Jim, I discovered, was rather embarrassed by the newsboys' strike. It made his paper look like some kind of Scrooge.

"You'll look worse," I said, "when we call a general labour boycott."

He was shocked: "But the newsboys don't belong to a union."

"You just wait. They will."

"Hold on a minute. You're not being fair. Give us to the end of the week."

The newsboys got their twenty cents a dozen, and I left with the impression that Jim Herder was a decent man in a job that demanded more toughness than he might be able to muster.

I saw him occasionally during the Confederation campaign when I was doing the editing and layout of *The Confederate*, while Smallwood was still doing most of the writing, and on one occasion I had joked, "You should hire me as an editor."

By the time I went to work for the Herders, Steve, Jim's nephew, was back from a stint with mainland newspapers, and had taken over the newsroom, intending to reorganize the editorial department along modern lines. Jim's older brother, Ralph, was president of the company, and another nephew, Hubert, was in charge of business and circulation. Ron Martin, the treasurer, was the only outsider with a share in the company. Like the Herders he was a man with solid middle-of-the-road business sense, and a strain of kindliness and generosity.

"Do you intend to make a career of journalism?" Jim Herder asked me during my interview.

"I've always intended to make writing my life work," I told him. "Politics was never my main interest."

"I see. And how long will it be before you rush off to one of the big papers on the mainland?"

"I'll make you a promise," I said. "Take me on, and I'll stay for at least two years."

So from being a temporary reporter doing piece work in the House of Assembly, I moved to a full-time job in the newsroom.

The Herders were not popular with all of their employees, but my own relationship with them couldn't have been better. They treated me with unfailing respect and consideration, and gave me great freedom to express my own ideas in the paper, even though my political opinions were far to the left of their own. Steve Herder in particular was an outspoken fan of my writing; I in turn had deep respect for his sense of how a newspaper should be run. Steve and I also happened to share a love of the outdoors, and were committed conservationists.

I never asked for a raise in pay, but I got raises anyway. They also gave me unasked-for bonuses when I produced special issues such as the trouting and travel supplements, on which I did most of the writing and editing, and some of the photography. After one of those specials came out, Jim would call me into his office and say, "Here's a little something to express our thanks." Inside the envelope would be a cheque for $100 or $150. I was soon earning between $7,000 and $8,000 a year, which, for a single young man in the 1950s, was very good money indeed. On such an income I could go on foreign vacations or on summer voyages to Labrador, buy expensive fishing gear and boats (I owned an aluminum outboard and a "convertible" cruiserette which I bought off the floor of a boat exhibition in Toronto). I put a bit of money into an investment fund (which failed to grow as it was supposed to do) and bought two endowment policies from an insurance company.

It was a curious association between a family of respectable Gladstone Liberals and a far-out radical, only recently a labour organizer who had introduced such devilish devices as the rotating strike, and who was suspected in some quarters of being a communist.

It was the McCarthy era, when guilt by association was widely accepted, when Canada was completely committed to the cause of helping the Americans to achieve worldwide hegemony, when any deviation from right-of-centre politics was treason, when "peacenicks" and "parlour pinks" were regarded as unfit for any kind of paid employment. My associations were of the worst: some of Canada's most prominent communists were my personal friends. I knew Albert McLeod so well that I stayed at his house when I visited Toronto, and went with him to various functions of the political left, including performances of Greek plays at Massey Hall, and a convention of the Canadian Peace Congress, at which I was the only reporter from a Canadian daily newspaper or news agency. The commitment of Canada's press to the Cold War was virtually total.

This was the first test of my relationship with the Herders. Naturally, the spooks of the RCMP got word back to them of what dangerous company I was keeping in Toronto, and after one of my trips Jim Herder mentioned this to me.

"Sure," I said, "there are communists in the peace congress and in the labour movement. Some of them are my personal friends. But the reports I sent back to the paper were straight, weren't they?"

"Just so," he said. "Don't let it bother you."

So I continued to have the *Canadian Tribune*, the Canadian communist weekly, delivered to my office as an antidote to the grossly slanted reporting of the Canadian Press, Associated Press, and Reuters. When I had time to do it, I also edited the wire copy that we received, deleting the passages that were too obviously written by front-line soldiers in the Cold War. *The Evening Telegram* was one of the very few Canadian dailies to oppose the rearmament of Germany. We did this as a matter of set policy, with which the owners of the paper agreed. The editor of the *Ottawa Citizen* was fired for doing the same thing. Fifteen years before its hour had struck, *The Telegram* was suggesting that détente between east and west ought to be possible. Throughout the 1950s, the attitudes of almost every other daily newspaper in Canada seemed to be handed straight down from the military-industrial complex that was fattening itself on the Cold War, south of the border. Canadians, I believe, have forgotten what biased reporting of the news they took for granted in the 1950s.

But of course we were not mainly concerned with international politics. The misdeeds of the Newfoundland government were much closer to home, and, with Smallwood as government spokesman, were almost excessively visible. It is hardly an exaggeration to say that he was on the front page every day. With this formidable foe we were soon embroiled in dubious battle.

Because the opposition in the House of Assembly was inexperienced and numerically weak, I tried to give its members every possible break. No opposition politician ever complained of my reporting. Not so the government. Don Jamieson, a Liberal-come-lately who had switched his allegiance the moment Smallwood was in power, phoned and threatened to sue me because I had reported in too interpretive a manner opposition remarks about the way he was squeezing the juice from his first political plum, the "Buy Newfoundland" campaign. Joey had placed the campaign in Don's keeping, believing him to be, above everything, an expert salesman.

"You go right ahead and sue," I said, and hung up the phone. It was the attitude that both I and *The Telegram* were to maintain over the next six years, when my reporting and editing were to cause endless threats of suits, a threat of imprisonment for "breach of privilege of the House," three writs for libel, one dramatic court trial, and a threat from the government to have the paper padlocked. I felt, and the management agreed, that you should never back down when you were right, and that the first rule for an interpretive reporter was to interpret, fairly but fearlessly.

The Telegram, during my years as reporter, columnist and editor, was still a fighting journal, one of the last in Canada. Public injustice and stupidity, blatant graft and corruption, the evils of the social system, could all get us fighting mad. We were still living in the era of *The Front Page*. Reporters were newshounds and foot-sloggers, with their "beats" and their private "sources." The scoop was a major achievement, and if something "broke" after we'd gone to press, we stopped the presses, did a remake, and ran a second edition, usually with a top foreign story on page one replaced by the new local story. If we were lucky, and if the Rube Goldberg contraption in the press room behaved itself, we would not have to stop the press for more than fifteen or twenty minutes before it was rolling with the new edition. There were times, though, when the thing didn't behave itself, but decorated the walls and ceilings with strips of newsprint like tossed rolls of toilet tissue. Those were the times when the hair of Hedley Tuff, the gentlemanly production manager, turned a whiter shade of grey.

Steve Herder had inherited the department little changed from the time when Smallwood himself had worked there. Pat O'Reilly, the "other" reporter in Joey's time, still wrote his stories in longhand on scraps of newsprint the size of postcards, and searched the files daily for titbits from fifty years ago. As time went on, and O'Reilly gained confidence in me, he passed more and more of his news tips over to me for treatment in depth.

Mark Ronayne, the feature writer, hammered out lead after lead until he caught the ultimate sense of drama from yesterday's forest fire or trawler sinking, then skipped out for a straightener at the pub across the street. Mark paraded his cynicism. "Never forget that you're a hack writer," he told me. Mark and Steve and I shared many a round of beers in the noisy barroom of what was then called the Crosbie Hotel. But Mark wasn't happy at the paper. He later went to work—still as a hack writer—for the Department of the Environment in Ottawa, where I met him once or twice, and we shared a few more beers.

Eric Seymour, senior to Mark, wrote headlines for the wire copy, did a mild-mannered daily column, and reviewed books. He had formerly edited local news as well, but Steve took over this job himself, and later passed most of it along to me. He soon took the title "Managing Editor" and gave me the title of "Associate Editor," which meant that I was associate to him, not to C.E.A. Jeffrey, who was Editor, with sole responsibility for the editorial page, and for nothing else

We had a women's editor, too, Doris Power. Women newspaper readers were supposed to have very narrow interests, so most of the "women's page" consisted of social notes, accounts of weddings, and recipes. Doris also wrote a column, and brought such flair to her menial job that she won a national newspaper award for her work.

These, along with the sports editor, were the core of the department. Casual reporters came and went, rarely stayed for long: the pay was low, and the job was demanding. With little or no supervision they were expected to dig up and write news stories that were fresh and exciting. Rarely were they assigned anything specific. They were essentially on their own, attempting to do work that demanded both imagination and creativity. Better-paid jobs in industry or government awaited anyone who showed a glimmer of talent. One of our reporters became a *Time* magazine editor, and later assistant to the Prime Minister. Another went to work for the College of Fisheries. A third became host of the most controversial open-line show in the Atlantic provinces. A fourth, after a long intervening career as reporter and foreign correspondent, became editor of *Saturday Night*. Few remained full-time professional writers.

We worked with minimum equipment: war surplus typewriters that had served desk soldiers on the American bases in the 1940s, a single teletype link with Canadian Press, one battered dictionary suitable for high school. But I soon began asking for, and getting, numerous improvements. These included a direct telephone line to the newsroom, bypassing the switchboard, an ultra-light portable typewriter for use on aircraft, a Rolleiflex camera for feature work, supplementing the two 4x5 Speed Graphics already in use, and a library of reference books. In such small ways the twentieth century began to invade Newfoundland newsrooms.

On a paper the size of *The Telegram* (press run 30,000 in the early fifties, rising to twice that within the decade) a reporter did just about everything except set type. A few months after I started working there I was not only writing copy, but editing it, headlining it, and seeing it through makeup in the composing room. Once or twice, I wrote every story on page three—the main local news page—edited my own copy, wrote the headlines, made up a half-size dummy, then stood across the composing bench while Dick Squires, the chief compositor, fitted slugs from the linotypes into the steel forms, consulted me about last minute cuts when a story was a shade too long, locked up the whole thing, and sent it to be rolled into a matte for casting. Though the material was already proofed and corrected, we nevertheless reread the matts to make sure there wasn't a gross error such as a misplaced headline.

Since there was no Saturday paper in the 1950s, and we were

always on the street by noon, the editorial department had blissful two-and-a-half-day weekends. Then Dick Squires and I would head off with tents and canoes and at least one bottle of rum for a couple of days of trout fishing. We were occasionally joined in our wilderness excursions by one of the pressmen, or one of the photographers, but more often by Bob Forsey, son of one of Joey's cabinet ministers, and a neighbour of his named Harold Taylor, both of them still schoolboys. On those weekend expeditions we caught a disgraceful number of trout—rarely less than two or three dozen each. At least once we pooled the largest specimens from our various catches and won a prize in an annual fishing contest. We also displayed them in photographs in the trouting supplements.

That the aging Editor, C.E.A. Jeffrey, had responsibility for the editorial page, and for nothing else, was an arrangement rarely understood by the public. People were always phoning Mr. Jeffrey looking for free publicity for their pet projects, or complaining that they had received bad coverage from some reporter, and then feeling that they were getting the brush-off when their calls were transferred to some anonymous news editor—Steve or Eric Seymour, or myself. Even Smallwood seemed to blame Jeffrey, to some extent, for my daily attacks on the government.

Gradually, things changed. Gradually the Peter Principle took over. I began contributing editorials from time to time, and then frequently, to the editorial page, and when Mr. Jeffrey retired I took over his desk. It was a nice desk, in a nice big office, with books around, and a carpet underfoot, but it didn't please me all that much. I was never one-tenth as good pontificating in the leaders as I was revealing the government's latest dirty tricks in my column. The editor's office now became for the first time an integrated part of the editorial department. I wrote my leaders after consultation with the managing editor, and sometimes with other members of management. Eventually, we began having a conference each morning to decide the shape of the following day's editorial page.

By now I was involved in a mass of desk work—editing, headlining, writing leaders, laying out pages, putting "specials" together, as well as writing my daily column. It left me virtually no time for the job I could do best—feature writing.

My column "Political Notebook," the major force in Newfoundland journalism in the 1950s, had been born at Smallwood's suggestion.

"Look Harold," he said one day, "a lot of things go on in the House that aren't exactly news but ought to be reported. Why don't you do a daily column?"

He had in mind a column of chit-chat. He little imagined what a Frankenstein's monster he was creating. When I reminded him of this conversation about thirty years later, he exclaimed, "Well... God forgive me! I should have bit my tongue!"

Within a year I was Smallwood's principal opposition. Scandals, skulduggery, inside information that had leaked through my private pipeline from cabinet meetings, as well as my attacks on government policies, all wound up in the 1200-word daily spectacular on the top of page three. I produced such an endless string of sensations that people bought the paper for the column alone. Circulation soared. More than ninety percent of surveyed readers said they read the column before anything else in the paper. Some even said they read nothing except the column and the comics. Joey spent six years trying to plug the leaks, and fired one minister who was suspected of being a personal friend of mine, but he never managed to stop the flow of information. It never occurred to him to look in the offices of the police department, which was one of my most fruitful sources.

When the government turned its big guns on me the Herders got their backs up, not only because I was a great asset to the paper, but because they felt they had a tradition of independence and ethics to maintain—the tradition of the founder, Steve Herder's grandfather, who had gone to jail for his principles when he refused to divulge the name of a correspondent, and had sat in his cell in his underwear, refusing to put on the prison uniform. The four Herders who were at *The Telegram* in my time never showed the slightest inclination to bow to government pressure.

While Jim oversaw the general business of the paper, and Steve worked to transform it into a hard-nosed, modern journal, Hubert tried to build it into an efficient, expanding business, operating throughout the province as no daily paper had done, up to that time.

The transformation was spectacular. While I was there he added a fleet of vans to the circulation department, installed a press with four times the capacity of the old one, introduced electronic engraving on plastic, then computer typesetting, and finally photo-makeup that almost eliminated typesetting altogether.

We opened a bureau in central Newfoundland with its own daily distribution system, and succeeded in expanding daily distribution to a range of more than two hundred miles from St. John's. We installed teletype hook-ups to Grand Falls, Gander and Corner Brook, and ran a daily news exchange with the Corner Brook *Western Star*, bought from the Bowater Corporation when it came up for sale. I was posted to Corner Brook briefly as manager of the *Star* while its permanent manager was out of the province.

In the midst of this expansion I suggested adding a light aircraft to our transportation fleet. I might have got it, had Newfoundland's flying weather been more reliable, but such a plane might have been grounded at Torbay for weeks at a stretch. The expansion rate was almost frantic. While our circulation doubled, the number of pages to an issue increased three times, and there was a constant demand for new recruits to the editorial staff.

It wasn't all smooth. One reporter from the Mainland that we hired on sight, without references, turned out to be an ex-convict whose journalistic ethics came straight from the Mafia. A sports editor who drank more than even a hardened news hound could handle freaked out in the small hours of the morning and tore the telephone wires out of the walls. There is also a story to the effect that he threw a typewriter out of a third-story window, but I don't think that part of it is true. His successor was a quiet, competent young man who, one dark night, drove his car into an unlighted excavation on a city street, and was killed.

What about editorial quality? The selection of news? I don't think we ever considered the difference between real news and the pseudo-event. Our pages were filled with such pseudo-events, most of them overblown government announcements of impending developments that were to transform Newfoundland into the image of Chicago and Detroit. All of it was accepted as fact. The villages of Donovans, Gander, Come-by-Chance, LaScie, and Bay d'Espoir were, in turn, promoted into imaginary cities with industrial populations of hundreds of thousands.

We continued to publish this pie-in-the-sky under eight-column headlines, as though we believed it. Though we opposed the government, we continued to treat its political propaganda as "news." I suppose a truly reflective, truly responsible newspaper, would have relegated such nonsense to the back pages, next to the astrology column, with some such heading as "Latest Government Announcements," cautioning its readers, in its editorial columns, to treat it all with scepticism.

The pseudo-event helped to keep Smallwood in power for nearly a quarter of a century. He was a gifted manipulator of the news media. C.D. Howe, Sir William Stevenson, Edmund de Rothschild, Randolph Churchill and Eleanor Roosevelt, among others, were paraded before the press cameras to make dreams appear real. Smallwood managed to use *The Telegram*, which opposed him, almost as effectively as he used the chain of radio and TV stations owned by Don Jamieson, Geoff Stirling, and other loyal Liberals.

The Telegram's failings in this regard, I am convinced, were the result of human limitations, not of any willingness to deceive the public, or of any conscious decision to allow the paper to be used by politicians for such deception. The Herders and their editors were trying to be fair to all sides, within the limits of bourgeois liberalism, and sometimes this could be misused by clever manipulators who, in their turn, believed firmly in what they were doing, and were even, perhaps, deceived by their own dreams.

Only three or four pages of the paper contained local news or locally written comment. There was also church news, sports reporting, women's news, and the like—another three or four pages. The rest was filled with advertising, the spaces between the ads stuffed with low-grade wire copy and syndicated materials that added little to the paper's appeal. There was, however, a real effort to add local columns of special interest. One contributor wrote a local column on astronomy. Another did a weekly article on the care of pets. A third did humorous writing with a strongly local flavour.

International news was poorly covered, much of it Cold War propaganda. The great scientific breakthroughs of the fifties, and the social revolutions of the sixties, were scarcely reported at all. This was hardly the fault of the paper's editors. Much more, it was the fault of Canadian Press, whose judgment of news was consistently moronic. The discovery of the structure of DNA rated a single paragraph. The first heart transplant was treated like the second coming.

Even our beautiful "specials," locally written and photographed, were only stuffing between ads. Ads for fishing gear filled up a spring issue; Winchesters and CIL ammunition fattened one in autumn; every summer I produced, single-handed, a supplement filled with my own wanderings about the province, and my own photographs of its attractions, the spaces filled with advertising by hotels and caterers. At least in those days the supplements were staff-written, so that the advertisers got something decent for their money. Later, they were not. The ads remained, but the filling became syndicated garbage from the Mainland, often completely irrelevant to Atlantic Canada.

The fifties were the glorious years of opposition journalism. The Ottawa Liberals had been in power almost as long as the Pope, seemed just as immovable, and were fair game for anyone with a slingshot.

What Judith Robinson did to the federal Liberals in the Toronto *Telegram*, I did to the provincial Liberals in the St. John's *Telegram*. In addition, I dug up every possible scrap of scandal, polished it until it shone like a black diamond, and published it on page three.

Judith and I were great friends. In addition to a taste for French bread, blue cheese, red wine, and travel, we shared a common opposition to Smallwood, Pickersgill, and that gruesome old man, C.D. Howe. There were marked differences in the way we worked: Judith was almost always on speaking terms with her victims, but sometimes not with her editors, who were known to mutilate her columns, or even kill them. I was always on the friendliest terms with the Herders, but Smallwood had ceased speaking to me by 1954. His aversion was so intense that he had the whole press gallery barred from the afternoon tea club in the House of Assembly, an informal get-together of press and politicians founded and financed by the reporters. In retaliation, the Press Club, of which he was honourary president, expelled him from its membership.

In the 1950s the government did not have its own printing plant, but farmed out its work to job plants in St. John's. *The Telegram* had the best job printing plant in the province. Somebody—I never learned who—approached the Herders with a proposition. Drop me from their staff, and they could have the government's entire printing contract. Hubert Herder, the business manager, whose department would have benefitted enormously from the government contract, responded by composing a front-page editorial with the title "Along the Street Called Straight," and refused to accept any more government advertising. It was the only writing I ever knew Hubert to do.

In the succeeding election campaign Smallwood phoned to ask if the ban on government advertising extended to a ban on advertising by the Liberal Party. It did not, of course. There was no way a public newspaper could accept advertising from one political party and not from another. So the Liberals ran full-page ads in the columns of their implacable foe. This made sense, from their point of view, because *The*

Telegram reached more than twice as many readers as any other daily paper in Newfoundland.

In general, advertisers were discouraged from trying to influence editorial policies. Not that they never tried it. But Steve Herder was very jealous of editorial independence, and since he was an important shareholder without being involved in the paper's business affairs, he was in a strong position to tell the advertising department to stay in its own back yard. Occasionally they asked our advice on a question of ethics, but I cannot recall that they ever suggested that we should play down a story distasteful to their big accounts. This fact is one I've found most difficult to have accepted by outsiders. Almost without exception, they assumed that the paper was at the beck and call of its advertisers, and were sceptical of my assurances that it was not.

We tried to allocate space fairly. Statements by the Federation of Labour and the Board of Trade got the same kind of play. Developers and their critics were treated impartially unless we were convinced that we had to take sides in the public interest. We succeeded in stopping one housing development that was dangerously close to Windsor Lake, and was certain to pollute the watershed of Beachy Cove Brook, which we regarded as an important bit of wilderness close to the city. In this I had the strong backing of Steve Herder, who regarded small rivers as almost sacred, and of Ed Roberts, then a junior minister in the Smallwood government.

We won a number of other conservation battles, too: we managed to save the old lighthouses at Cape Spear and Ferryland after the government had ordered them destroyed. We prevented the mass spraying of insecticides in the Newfoundland forests at a time when DDT was still regarded as mankind's greatest blessing. We prevented the use of sprays altogether in provincial parklands at a time when neighbouring provinces, notably New Brunswick, were blanketing themselves in a fog of poisons.

Until 1954 the only artists at *The Telegram* were in the advertising department. Sometimes one would produce a cartoon or news illustration, but usually they were too busy. Then we hired an editorial artist, Bill Werthman, who turned out local cartoons, drew illustrations for features, and finally drew our own daily comic strip.

To write the strip I secured Newfoundland's most gifted story teller, Ted Russell, who had been having a pretty thin time since leaving Smallwood's government. To eke out a living Russell had turned to story telling on CBC, had invented Uncle Mose and the *Tales from Pigeon Inlet* that made him posthumously famous. Russell re- wrote the material into comic sequence, Werthman drew it, and the engraving machine turned it into a "scancut" for the press. It was the sort of expensive "frill" that made *The Telegram* an exciting paper in the fifties and the sixties. The money spent on that strip could have filled our back pages with all the most popular syndicated strips in North America, every one of them produced in the United States, and carrying a powerful shot of American culture to the Canadian dailies that ran them because they were cheap and popular. We ran them too, of course, but be also gave the Newfoundland people something of their own for their entertainment.

Meanwhile I was locked in battle with Joey and his minions. (I noted that his minions often enjoyed my columns on the sly, grinning wickedly behind his back as they perused Political Notebook in the House of Assembly, a thing none would have dared to do before his face). His first response was to attack *The Telegram* for breach of privilege.

According to the old British precedents on which Canadian parliamentary practice is based, a reporter or editor who misquotes, misinterprets, or brings Members of the House into disrepute, may be hailed before the bar of the House and committed to jail without trial for the balance of the legislative session. At least once in the history of Newfoundland this rule was actually invoked; a man who insulted a Member of the House was jailed for breach of privilege; his lawyer, and a judge who issued a writ of *habeas corpus* on his behalf, were also imprisoned. This was the sort of precedent that Joey had in mind when he attacked *The Telegram* for its reporting of the House.

The catch is that a committee of the House must bring in a report on privilege, and to prevent a purely political decision, the committee must include at least one member from the opposition. There was no way any member of the opposition was going to vote to send me to jail. The committee set up to "put Horwood behind bars, where he belongs" as Joey described it, never brought in a report.

Next came the libel suits. First from the Minister of Welfare because of the interpretive way in which I had reported one of his speeches—"Wives Exchanged Like Chattels!" the headlines screamed—the very words the minister had let slip in describing an outport filled with jacketars, Newfoundland's Metis, who did not share his Wesleyan views on sex. He had added that the children should be taken from their parents to be "decontaminated." I had said in my report that though the minister did not name the place, he was actually talking about Stephenville. There was, indeed, a very slight slip here. I should have said "the Stephenville area," because what he actually had in mind was the rural community, rather than the people of the town itself, which had mushroomed from construction work during war time. The distinction, however, was a nice one, and he had referred in his speech to "a tale of three towns."

It would hardly be an exaggeration to say that all hell broke loose. We were not only served with writs. We were denounced, by Smallwood and others, as Tory lickspittles willing to go to any length to discredit the government. The welfare officer at Stephenville handed in his resignation. The Mayor of Stephenville demanded to know, if the minister was not talking about Stephenville, then what Newfoundland town he was talking about. After all, he had said "town," not "place" or "area."

The Corner Brook *Western Star*, which carried my reports verbatim, was under greater pressure than *The Telegram*. It had a large circulation in Stephenville, and it carried libel insurance. It published a retraction and an apology, without consulting me—I would never have consented to such a course. *The Telegram* management agreed with me. The minister could see us in court, where our lawyer would repeat the demand made by the mayor of Stephenville to know what town, in heaven's name, he had in mind. When it came to the push, the minister backed off. He continued, despite the suit, to be a friend of mine, and many years later I had the pleasure of recommending him for a Canada Council grant.

Next came suits from two business firms that had been embroiled in Smallwood's economic development schemes. We judged in one case that we had overstepped the mark a trifle, and published a correction (not an apology) which the firm agreed to accept. In the other case we knew that the company had been involved in graft up to its eyeballs, and we were prepared to prove it. When they saw we were going to fight the case, they withdrew.

The day after one of our most highly publicized libel suits had been thrown out of court I went to a flower shop to buy a carnation to wear to the press gallery in the House of Assembly.

"Here! It's free!" the proprietor exulted, "You can have a dozen if you want."

I sat in the front row that day wearing my carnation and grinning provokingly while the government fumed, the attorney general muttered darkly about investigations for criminal libel, and the opposition made cracks about things being laughed out of court.

In fact, we had a lot of information that we never used. We never attacked government members on personal grounds, though heaven knows some of them were vulnerable enough. One of them had fathered illegitimate children whom he left to be supported by welfare. Another had been a gunman in the United States, and had served a term for armed robbery. We had documentation on a series of business deals that may not have been exactly illegal, but would certainly have been highly embarrassing, if published. They did not, however, involve public money, and so far as I know, the documents are still locked in *The Telegram's* vault.

When I discovered proof that the German promoters of one of Joey's new industries had been robbing the government, I sent word to him that we had information that he ought to know about. He sent word back that he wouldn't talk to me, but that he'd be willing to see one of the Herders. But the information didn't seem to take him by surprise. He must have known, by then, that he'd been taken for a multi-million-dollar ride by a bunch of sharpers. Not many months later the rubber factory at Holyrood, which had turned to making leaky rubber boots when the local priest refused to allow it to manufacture birth control devices, closed its doors, and the remains of its inventory went up in a pillar of smoke that could be seen from a hundred miles out in the Atlantic.

We caught the Minister of Supply and his brother, a small merchant, selling goods to a government agency at well above market value. I was especially angry about this incident because the goods were destined for northern Labrador, where the people could least afford to be victimized by such robbery. I called the minister and his brother a pair of grafters, and waited for the writs to be delivered. They never arrived. And instead of resigning from the government, as in all decency he should have, the minister was merely transferred to a less sensitive department.

Finally the whole government, all thirteen ministers, sued *The Telegram* for the way we handled the Germaine Plante scandal. Plante was a high-priced Montreal call girl brought to Newfoundland to set up a service for visiting VIPs and economic developers. She had been hired by the ex-minister who was also an ex-convict, one of Smallwood's closest associates (he later died while Canada was trying to extradite him from the United States for yet another criminal offence). Plante's base of operations was a nightclub owned by Liberal members of the House of Assembly, and run by a party man. No direct connection with the government, beyond this, was ever proven. You couldn't say that the cabinet had actually passed a minute of council to bring her to St. John's. But the implications were obvious.

Miss Plante defected, claiming that she had been scandalously short-changed, and was spirited off by a reporter to a boarding house in a quiet part of town. From her hideaway she continued to issue statements that made headlines, day after day. Besides her knowledge of the proposed prostitution ring, she had knowledge, she said, of a conspiracy to defraud the federal government of the excise tax on some ten thousand gallons of liquor. The government, and the police, went frantic trying to lay hands on her, and *The Telegram* had a romping old time publishing her accusations. When she finally surfaced she was tried for attempted extortion.

Meanwhile, *The Telegram* was sued by the thirteen ministers of the Crown. When the sheriff arrived to serve the writs, I was in Jim Herder's office. By now he was hardened to this kind of thing. "What!" he said, looking up from his desk with a grin, "Not you again!"

The trial turned into a battle between two of Newfoundland's leading lawyers, J.B. McEvoy for the plaintiffs, and Robert S. Furlong (later Chief Justice) for the defence. After hearing legal arguments for a whole day, the judge threw out the case and dismissed the jury, awarding costs to *The Telegram*. The matter did not end there. The plaintiffs ignored the order to pay costs, and *The Telegram* then entered a civil suit for collection. We won that suit, too. But so far as I know, we still didn't collect.

Those were heady times, with reports of former Gestapo agents loose in the land, and at least one political kidnapping. The era ended, in a sense, with the fall of Dr. Alfred Valdmanis, Joey's right-hand man, who had been wished on him by C.D. Howe, and who turned out to be a former Latvian Quisling who had served under Hitler. But the wheelings and dealings didn't stop after Valdmanis had gone to jail. It is interesting to note that throughout the full length of his career in government, Smallwood was closely associated with criminals, but always managed to keep his own nose clean.

Then the seemingly impossible happened: in 1957 the Liberal monolith in Ottawa was toppled. A cabal of journalists calling itself the Committee for the Salvation of Canadian Democracy had worked to bring down the government. I was a member of that group, having been recruited by Judith Robinson. The group had its own funds, raised by a sub-committee, and was not connected with the Progressive-Conservative organization. Among other activities we ran a series of radio spots using our own copy and our own names across Canada. We did not believe in the government's invulnerability, as most TV and radio journalists did.

I can still remember vividly the screaming incredulity of the TV reporters on election night watching the Liberal Indispensables, who had been in power longer than most of them could remember, going down to defeat. Even Howe was beaten in his own riding by a young CCF teacher named Doug Fisher.

Diefenbaker, elected by a plurality, invited me to Ottawa, but I never seriously considered going, even though I knew I was getting stale as a journalist. I was now handling the editorial page, unable to make it sparkle like Political Notebook, and many of my concerns (like the battle against budworm spraying) were far ahead of their time.

In some matters, though, I had quick and unexpected success, as happened when I set out to stop the dumping of waste oil into the sea, then a legal procedure.

One day after I'd been working at *The Telegram* for perhaps two years Les Tuck walked into my office and announced: "I'm going to turn you into a naturalist." Tuck was a self-made scientist, employed by the federal government as field biologist in Newfoundland. Birds were his specialty, but he was interested in every aspect of ecology, especially of Newfoundland and the Arctic.

He was good copy, his activities in the field always newsworthy, his relations with reporters friendly and helpful. He began inviting me on field trips and teaching me the game of bird watching. Almost before I knew it, I was hooked, and began keeping a life list in my *Peterson*.

With Tuck I got into such unlikely places as the Sandy Lake barrens, far to the south of Badger, where we photographed a caribou herd and a sleeping black bear, Tuck sneaking up on the animal, setting up his tripod, and waiting for the bear to awaken before starting to run his 16 mm film. He was very brave in the presence of such big animals, including stag caribou in rut, because I was supposed to be standing by with a loaded .303 rifle, ready to defend him in case he was attacked. In fact, I had often left the rifle on the ground, and crept forward with him to try to get some still shots with a Speed Graphic.

Once he had me hooked on nature, he proposed that we launch a campaign to put an end to oil dumping, which was then killing millions of sea birds, and doing untold other damage to the marine and coastal environment. It was standard practice, at that time, for oil tankers, having delivered a load of crude oil, to flush out their tanks at sea, leaving the waste oil floating on the surface. In some places they could not do this inside coastal waters, but they could do it everywhere once they were more than three miles offshore.

With Tuck's help I wrote feature articles, illustrated with photographs of dead seabirds floating up on the shore, spot news stories of the latest oil spills, and followed them up with editorials and columns demanding that the senseless destruction of the wildlife and the environment be stopped. Some of the articles were spread across two pages with eight-column headlines and photographs. Tuck clipped all this copy and sent it off to his superiors in Ottawa, who saw to it that the articles were photocopied and sent to the right ministers and their deputies.

It worked like magic. Within months—not years, but months—Parliament was debating a law to make it illegal for any ship to dump oil within two hundred miles of the coastline of Canada, with powers of arrest and stiff penalties for violators. Soon there were a few arrests, and soon afterwards word got around that you'd better not dump waste oil within two hundred miles of the coast of Canada. Tuck and I drank each other's health, and were joined by Steve Herder. But it was a brief triumph in the midst of—for me—increasing disenchantment.

By now, it seemed, I was entrenched as an institution, one of those old editors who will never dry, but just blaze away. I could look forward to another thirty-five affluent years, and then the gold watch.

But Farley Mowat came to town. We took an instant liking to each other, and he began to hint that I was wasting my time working for a provincial daily. Late in the summer of 1958 I drove to Stephenville Airport and met Mowat for a camping and drinking tour of Newfoundland. The day the tour ended, I handed in my resignation.

It was 1958. Summer. I sold my cruiser, my aluminum skiff, my two outboard motors, took my tent and canoe and headed into the wilderness alone. It was perhaps the worst time of the year (barring winter) for canoeing, but there was enough water in the Indian River to float my light boat over most of the shallows. The experience was one I made use of again and again in my later writing. I was gone a week. When I returned to St. John's I had the beginning of a beard. Then I went camping for another week, in a part of the Goulds that could be reached only by boat. I spent those two weeks almost entirely alone, and made the discovery that I was a compulsive writer. No matter where I was I needed a pad and a pencil. Nothing gave me such true satisfaction as the sentences and paragraphs I put together. But I wasn't going back to newspapers. Somehow or other, I'd make it as a freelancer, and begin writing books.

My association with *The Telegram* did not end in 1958. Two years later, as a freelancer, I began contributing a weekly nature column, "Outside Information," and illustrating it with my own drawings. Some of it, I later reworked into my book *The Foxes of Beachy Cove*. I continued writing that column for about ten years, and it became a crusading vehicle for the environment, always a little ahead of its time, but not so far ahead that it failed in its purpose. I had learned to temper my blasts to the shorn public. The column had an enthusiastic public reception, and something rather like it has continued ever since. My brother Charles and my nephew John continued writing and illustrating a feature of this kind on behalf of the Natural History Society of Newfoundland. Their writing was less passionate and more scientifically based than mine.

In 1968, after my first two books had created a great sensation in Newfoundland (one of them a national bestseller, both winning national or international awards), I returned to *The Telegram* as a part-time feature writer. At least, that was the plan. I was to work half-time, around twenty hours a week, and was left almost entirely on my own. However, the Herders also wanted to use me as a kind of window dressing. They gave me the title of Associate Editor, and an office on the top floor with the management. What I didn't foresee was that this arrangement made me feel isolated, a kind of Writer in Residence, not quite part of the management team, and not quite part of the editorial department, either.

Ten years had made a great change in the paper. The newsroom was now a professional operation. The days of the newshound, the scoop, and the page one remake were now history. Steve Herder had moved up to management, and the editorial department was run by a keen young professional, Bob Innes, who had firm opinions on exactly how such a department should function. Innes seemed to be free of all editorial bias, interested only in presenting information, including other people's opinions, in as clear and attractive a form as possible. If he had any political or social opinions of his own, I never learned what they were. He had carried the work begun by Steve Herder to new levels.

The editorial staff had been enlarged; no one was expected to work on more than one story at a time, and reporters were encouraged to explore stories in depth if possible. We were no longer competing with radio, TV and other papers for spot news. Our job was to present the news in greater depth and detail than the electronic media could hope to do.

Ray Guy, an unhappy but devastatingly funny columnist, had been added as frosting to the daily cake. He was consistently funny at the government's expense, but he did not probe into their secret affairs and drag the skeletons out of their closets as I had done ten years earlier. His was in many ways a better, cleverer, more literary column then mine had ever been, but not nearly so damaging to those in power. Later he was to win the Leacock Award for a collection of his columns, and to add playwriting and acting to his repertoire.

The staff had become more literate. There were university graduates in English and history, and two people on their way to doctorates. Production had been streamlined, and there were great investments in new equipment: computers, teletypes, a photo-engraving department that could produce a 48-page paper daily on zinc plates. Circulation was still rising; the paper was getting bigger, and new features were being added every year.

And then the sky fell.

We woke up one morning to learn that the whole operation had been sold to the Thomson organization. From now on our ultimate boss would be that grinning Philistine, the Right Honourable Lord Thomson of Fleet, who had descended upon Canadian daily newspapers like the wolf on the fold. The Herders had expanded their two newspapers beyond the limits of their financing. It was either sell out or retrench. Thomson made them an offer they couldn't refuse, and the hundred-year-old family business was swallowed up, absorbed into the mainstream of homogenized garbage that the newspaper chains were spreading across Canada, coast to coast.

We were assured there would be no drastic changes—and there were not, for a while. The Thomson organization never meddled in the editorial policies of its papers. They were concerned only with money. If you could make money out of reading teacups, explaining biochemistry, or black magic, or a passionate love for Fidel Castro, it was all the same to them.

But you cannot dictate the financial affairs of a paper without interfering drastically, if indirectly, with its editorial content. The financial axework that began the day after the Thomson takeover soon had its effect. The print job deteriorated; the paper began to look cheap; before long, compared to the much smaller but still independent *Daily News*, it was a sleazy-looking production. Expensive services, such as the *New York Times* syndicate, that Innes had added to increase the quality of *The Telegram's* coverage, were dropped. Senior staff members who retired or resigned were replaced only by cub reporters.

The last time I saw Bob Innes I was already off the staff myself, living temporarily in Ontario, and back in St. John's for a visit. I found him in a mood bordering on despair. *The Telegram* had been his whole career, his life's work; he took great pride in the quality he had built into it, but in the past two years he had seen it slowly gutted under his feet; it was going the way of the Peterborough *Examiner*, and the other high-quality papers that had been swallowed by the giant corporations. Innes abandoned journalism, and went to work for a mining company. Guy, eventually, went the same way, but continued writing, for monthly magazines and TV.

To me, at least, that was the end of an era in St. John's. The city was now the sprawling metropolis that it has become today. Smallwood was in retirement, replaced by less able politicians. The mainland was moving in, converting St. John's into a Canadian city, even though the downtown core remained more European than Canadian. Memorial University still had its unique qualities, but the faculty was now an international body, with international roots, just a few departments such as English retaining the traditions that had been inherited from Memorial University College in the pre-Confederation days.

For myself, I was now living as much in mainland Canada as in the old city under Signal Hill. I spent three years on the faculty of one mainland university, and a fourth at another; I was twice vice-chairman of the Writers' Union of Canada, and became chairman in 1980, the same year I received the Order of Canada for literature, and became a personal friend of the Governor General. I wrote a string of successful books. My writing was published in China and Japan and other foreign places. But even then nearly everything I wrote was out of Newfoundland and Labrador, with more than a touch of nostalgia for the lost world in which I was born and raised, and abiding love for the unique city that sits between Mount Scio and The Narrows.